Londa Rohlfing

Sweatshirt Transformations

Sew
Jackets,
Vests &
Hoodies

8 Projects
from Cozy
to Elegant

C&T PUBLISHING

Text and Photography copyright © 2012
by Londa Rohlfing

Photography and Artwork copyright © 2012
by C&T Publishing, Inc.

Publisher: Amy Marson

Creative Director: Gailen Runge

Art Director: Kristy Zacharias

Editors: Liz Aneloski and Phyllis Elving

Technical Editors: Susan Nelsen and Amanda Siegfried

Cover Designer: April Mostek

Book Designer: Christina Jarumay Fox

Production Coordinator: Jessica Jenkins

Production Editor: Alice Mace Nakanishi

Illustrator: Aliza Shalit

Style Photography by Christina Carty-Francis and
Diane Pedersen of C&T Publishing, Inc., unless otherwise
noted; How-To Photography by Londa Rohlfing, unless
otherwise noted

Published by C&T Publishing, Inc., P.O. Box 1456,
Lafayette, CA 94549

Library of Congress Cataloging-in-Publication Data

Rohlfing, Londa, 1952-

Sweatshirt transformations : sew jackets, vests & hoodies
: 8 projects from cozy to elegant / Londa Rohlfing.

p. cm.

ISBN 978-1-60705-554-9 (pbk.)

1. Sweatshirts. 2. Jackets. 3. Sewing. I. Title.

TT649.R64 2012

646.4'5--dc23

2011046640

Printed in China

10 9 8 7 6 5 4 3 2 1

Contents

**Dedication and
Acknowledgments**...................4

Introduction...................5

Materials and Tools...................6

Why Start with a Sweatshirt?
Additional Fabrics • Basic Supplies

Basic Techniques...................8

Preparing the Sweatshirt • Two Fitting Techniques
Stabilizing the Neckline • Bias Strip Magic
Making Gathers • Setting Sleeves
Finishing the Edges • Fabric "Fur" Trim
Couching Basics

Projects

Adorned...................26

Carefree...................32

Amplified...................38

Promised...................46

Captured...................53

Innovative...................62

InVested...................72

Distinctive...................83

About the Author...................95

Dedication

I lovingly dedicate this book to my family, without whom my passion for sewing and business would never have been conceived.

My mother taught me to sew and says I grew up "under her sewing machine." Modeling the value of mother-hood enriched with a "sharing" hobby, she encouraged me as I struggled through projects while I learned the skills. Wisely putting me on a clothing allowance, she made sewing the obvious solution to satisfy my desire for clothes and more clothes through my teen years. My father modeled entrepreneurship—that working hard, putting the customer first, and honoring God in everything is the *only* way.

From the expensive machine purchased for me during our first year, through his wise consult during our retail store years, to using vacation time to "do shows" together, my husband has been by my side. I pray he will be there for many years to come.

My son has always been there with technical assistance, without which my business could never have grown and produced Talking Patterns. With frank design opinions, my daughter has consistently supported my work and has encouraged balance, through opportunities to *play* with my wonderful grandson.

Play is what it's all about. Artistic play is a gift from God and a glorifying thing to do. From my favorite author, Randy Alcorn: "It wasn't an accident that Jesus was born into a carpenter's family. Carpenters are makers. God is a maker. God made us his image-bearers, to be makers. When we die, we won't leave behind our creativity, but only what hinders our ability to honor God through what we create."

Acknowledgments

Since 1988, my life has crossed paths with many great people. National teachers have influenced and inspired me. Customers have become wonderful friends as together we've maneuvered sewing shows and guild and shop appearances around the country. Thanks to all of you from the bottom of my heart! I could *never* do this without your generous help and friendship. And without supportive customers worldwide, none of this would be possible … so thank you!

And … looking ahead to an exciting future with the publica-tion of this book, I am indebted to C&T Publishing and all of the wonderful editors who combined their amazing talents to make this dream come true.

I suppose it's like an orchestra. With God as the conductor, each of these people has been brought my way, in His perfect timing, to create the music of my life's work: teaching, supplying, and encouraging women in creative sewing.

I give to God my praise for gifting me as He desired and allowing me to honor Him as I use and share those gifts, both here and now and, prayer-fully, in the life to come.

Introduction

My goal in writing this book has been to encourage the development of your own creativity as you learn to design, fit, and embellish a stylish jacket made on a comfortable sweatshirt base. I actually *love* to write directions, so my hope is that this book will become a springboard for your creative garment sewing adventures. Even though I've chosen to create wearable art jackets based on sweatshirts, my designs and techniques certainly can be executed on *any* base fabric. I have done that myself, and I encourage you to do the same.

I have organized the information into three main sections. In Materials and Tools (page 6), I introduce you to some of my favorite sewing notions and equipment. As an avid seamstress for 46 years, many of them as a retailer and designer, I have certainly found tools I can't live without!

Over the last nine years and the creation of approximately 300 jackets, my techniques for embellishment, construction, and fitting have evolved through many stages. I'm thrilled for others to benefit from my learning process! You will find the methods I've learned in the chapter Basic Techniques (page 8), organized so that these can become your own good friends for creative sewing.

Finally, in the Projects section of the book, I offer specific directions for creating eight great jackets. These are organized according to skill level—easy, medium, and challenging. After reading through the Basic Techniques chapter and taking into account your own skills and experience, start with the level that seems best for you. Taking the time to sit and read (think) through the entire jacket directions is strongly suggested.

Integrated throughout the book are principles called out in Design Notes. These are just as important as the construction techniques. The goal isn't just to create a wonderful jacket, but for you to look spectacular in the jacket you make!

Above all, just dive in! After you've created a jacket following my directions, get started on *another* jacket, with the goal of being your own designer. It's almost impossible to ruin a sewing project, so set aside any fears and enjoy the process. If you happen to get stuck, my advice is to go take a shower and think creatively as the water massages your brain! Often just taking a break to walk around the house, or the block, will allow you to come up with a perfectly creative solution. I absolutely love to talk to creative sewers—if you need my help, just send me a quick email though my website at www.londas-sewing.com.

For me, the ultimate compliment is hearing, "I can't believe that is a sweatshirt!" or "Don't tell me you made that yourself!" Just get started, and you'll soon be grinning with pride over a job well done—and looking your very best in a creative jacket designed and made by *you!*

Materials and Tools

Why Start with a Sweatshirt?

Using a sweatshirt as a base gives you the recommended quality and fiber content in a range of colors you won't find in the same type of fabric sold by the yard—*and* you get great matching ribbing. Besides, sweatshirts are knits, and therefore very comfortable. The real fun comes in refining the fit and styling your own jacket.

The techniques in this book are designed to use with an 80% cotton / 20% polyester sweatshirt, *not* the cheaper 50% cotton / 50% polyester type.

USA Comfort Color Sweatshirts

Sized small through 3XL, these sweatshirts come in 40 colors, with more being added by the manufacturer. This brand includes pigment surface-dye colors *and* clear, bright colors from direct fiber reactive dyes that hold true longer. And they are dyed in the USA!

> **DESIGN NOTE**
>
> *Avoid a sweatshirt design that has a raglan sleeve—this style tends to exaggerate the hips. Also, be aware that the back neck locker patch on sweatshirts isn't always symmetrical, so don't assume that you can embellish this line.*

What Size?

The size of sweatshirt you need depends on which construction and fitting method you use to make your jacket—see Two Fitting Techniques (page 8).

Method 1

This method uses the existing sweatshirt construction as the basis of the jacket, so you'll want to purchase a sweatshirt that's just large enough to comfortably fit your largest measurement (bust, hips). Keep in mind the style of your jacket—will it close, or will it hang open?

Method 2

Think of the sweatshirt as yardage and matching ribbing. Purchase a size 3XL if you are a generous size to give yourself as much fabric to work with as possible.

Additional Fabrics

All of the jackets in this book call for decorative fabrics to use as trim or lining. This is what will make your jacket unique! You'll also need functional fabrics for interfacing and for making any alterations.

Decorative fabrics

These can be cotton, fashion, or home decorating fabrics. One of my favorites is silk dupioni, because its sheen provides a nice textural contrast to the rough sweatshirt surface.

Interfacing

Select an interfacing that provides structure—woven, knitted, or weft. Both fusible and sew-in types of interfacing work. Choose one with structure, such as Shape-Flex (C&T Publishing), and be sure to preshrink fusibles by soaking them in hot water until the water cools. Then lay them flat on a towel to dry.

Fleece

Polar fleece works perfectly for adding length to the body of your jacket and for making necessary alterations (see page 85).

Basic Supplies

You'll use the following notions for all of the projects in this book. Additional supplies and tools needed for individual jackets are listed with the project instructions.

Notions

100% polyester garment construction thread

This is important when sewing on a knit sweatshirt base that stretches, because the thread must stretch, too. Both Metrosene and Güterman 100% polyester threads are great. This is *not* shiny polyester machine embroidery thread, nor is it cotton quilting thread!

Monofilament thread

Use clear for light colors and smoke for dark colors, for invisible stitching, and especially for couching trim or yarn. Wonder Thread from YLI (nylon) comes on a cross-wound spool that feeds best with a small spool cap on a horizontal spool pin. MonoPoly from Superior Threads (polyester) comes on a parallel-wound spool that feeds best on a vertical spool pin.

Straight Fusible Stay Tape, Knit Fusible Stay Tape (www.londas-sewing.com)

This is called for in the directions for each jacket.

Essential Tools

The tools I use are listed below. The brand names and item numbers of my favorites are given in parentheses. All notions and tools are available from the author at www.londas-sewing.com.

- 4-in-1 Essential Sewing Tool (C&T Publishing) with seam ripper, stiletto, point turner, and presser

- 5-in-1 Sliding Gauge (Clover 9506, page 22)

- Fabric Chenille Brush (Fabric Café, page 24)

- Chalk marker (Chakoner, page 10)

- Small iron (Hobbico or Kandi)

- Machine needles (Schmetz stretch needles, sizes 75 and 90, and Schmetz twin stretch needle 4.0/75)

- Hand sewing needles (Clover 235) and darning needles (Chibi from Clover, 339 or 340, page 25)

- Pincushion (Ewesful wool)

- Glass-head pins (Clover 2501)

- Point turner/presser (Collins)

- Loop turner (Collins)

- Rotary cutter, ruler, and mat

- Scissors—both large dressmaker shears (Kai 5220) and duckbill appliqué scissors (page 23)

- Seam ripper (Clover 482/W)

- Serger (*optional*)

- Sewing machine with zigzag stitch adjustable in width and length

- Tissue paper (Medical Pattern Paper)

- Trolley Needle or pointed awl (page 25) (or 4-in-1 Essential Sewing Tool, listed at left)

- Ultimate 3-in-1 Color Tool (C&T Publishing)

> **tip**
>
> A dress form is a wonderful tool to have for making your jacket—but if you don't have one, ask a sewing friend to help you fit your garment. Directions for using duct tape to make a dress form double are available from Jean Haas (www.dressformdouble.com).

Basic Techniques

Preparing the Sweatshirt

1. Wash the sweatshirt to remove excess dye. Preshrink your embellishment fabrics.

2. Remove all the ribbings from the sweatshirt, cutting them off close to the seam with dressmaker shears on the sweatshirt side of the stitching. Don't worry that the cut edges are uneven.

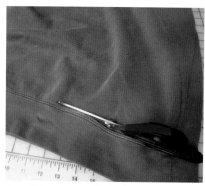

Cut off the sweatshirt ribbings.

3. Discard the neck ribbing; save the cuffs if you like the color. Using your rotary cutter and a ruler, trim away the seam from the bottom ribbing, cutting as close to the stitching as you can. A typical trimmed ribbing is 2″–2¼″ wide.

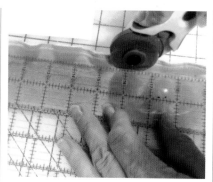

Trim the seam from the ribbing.

4. From inside the sweatshirt carefully cut out the layer of locker patch fabric below the back neck. Carefully rip out the seam. A stitching line will remain—a creative opportunity for concealment or embellishment. Using Method 2 (page 12) for fitting and construction usually eliminates this area.

Rip out the seam and carefully pull off the locker patch seam allowance.

Two Fitting Techniques

Choose whichever of the two fitting and construction methods works best for your body and for the jacket you're making. Some of the designs in this book specify one method or the other, while others can be made using either technique.

Either technique will work for the following jackets: *Amplified, Promised,* and *Innovative.*

Method 1 is required for the *Carefree* jacket, and Method 2 is necessary for the following jackets: *Adorned, Captured, InVested,* and *Distinctive. InVested* is a vest and includes specific instructions for fitting in the directions.

Whichever method you use, be sure to check your jacket instructions *first* to see if any variations in the following directions are required.

The Sweatshirt as Foundation

This fitting method uses the original sweatshirt construction, with some modifications, as the foundation of the jacket. Points to consider:

- Results are quick and easy.

- The sleeve-to-body seam remains in the dropped position, so there will be bulk under the armpit.

- If the sweatshirt isn't cut on perfectly straight grain, this method won't correct that.

- The fit will look better and the jacket will hang better on your body if you add shoulder pads, or use the foam "wear with everything" variety of shoulder pads.

What Size?

Keep the style of your jacket in mind—should it close completely, or hang open? Purchase a sweatshirt that's just large enough to comfortably fit the body's largest part (usually either the bust or the hips). Follow the directions for Preparing the Sweatshirt (page 8).

Shaping the Sweatshirt

1. If your sweatshirt doesn't have side seams, turn it inside out, lay it flat on an ironing surface, and press in "side seam" creases. Hand baste along these pressed lines with long stitches to mark the sides.

2. Locate the front center *at the neckline* by folding the sweatshirt in half, matching the front shoulder/yoke seams. Place a pin at the neckline to mark the center front. Do the same thing to find and mark the center back at the neckline.

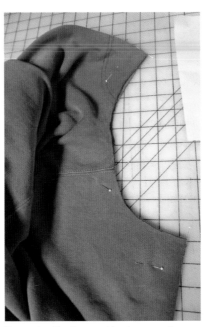

Determine the front and back center of the neckline.

3. Locate the front and back center *at the bottom edge* by folding the sweatshirt in half again, this time matching the pressed sides or side seams. Place pins on the bottom edge at the center front and center back.

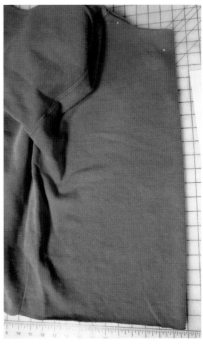

Determine center front and back at lower edge.

4. Fold the sweatshirt front from the neckline pin to the bottom edge pin; press in a center front crease. Make a center back crease the same way. Hand baste along this pressed line with long stitches to mark the center back.

5. Cut along the center front fold with your scissors. (Exception: The *Innovative* jacket design on page 62 features a side/front closure and should be cut according to the project directions.) Be sure to cut the neckline appropriately for the jacket you are creating. All necklines are found on the pattern tissue included in the pocket at the back of the book. Stabilize the cut edges with Straight Fusible Stay Tape, following the directions for your chosen jacket to determine whether the tape should be fused to the right side or wrong side of the sweatshirt.

6. Try on the sweatshirt, wrong side out, or fit it on a dress form. Keep in mind the thickness of the shirts you plan to wear under the jacket. To decrease the bagginess in the sleeves, pinch together and pin the excess fabric at the underarm seam. Generally this will be at least a 2″ pinch, which means 4″ of sleeve material will be removed.

Pin the extra sweatshirt fabric at the underarm seam.

7. Keeping your jacket style in mind, decide how much of the sweatshirt circumference you need to remove to achieve a flattering fit. Pin the sweatshirt to your pants at the center front. Pinch the excess fabric together at the center front and sides; pin, distributing the extra material equally.

DESIGN NOTE

If the side seams of your sweatshirt swing toward the back and the center back rides up higher than the sides, Method 2 (page 12) will work better for your body type. You may need to make a full-back alteration (page 13).

8. If the sweatshirt is too loose in the back, the center back basting line is now vitally important to create a center back seam or a long released tuck (appropriate for *Promised*). A huge angled dart underneath the fabric embellishment is substituted in *Amplified*.

Pin the excess fabric at the center back.

9. On one side, mark the new continuous side/underarm seamline you've pinned, using a chalk marker on the *wrong* side of the sweatshirt. If you want a turned-back cuff, make sure the sleeve width is constant (not tapered) for about 7″ above the wrist edge.

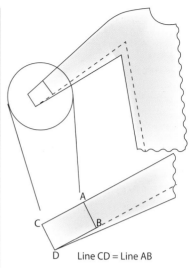

Line CD = Line AB

The dotted line shows the new stitching line, with an equal-width area for turning the cuff.

Chalk the new stitching line along the side and sleeve.

10. Stitch along the chalked seamline using a stretch size 75 needle in your sewing machine. Your stitch length should be a little longer than normal to accommodate the thick fabric. Trim, leaving a ⅜″ seam allowance. Save the cutoff material to use as a template for the second side.

If you will be adding embellishment on the shoulder, the back, and the sleeves, mark and stitch the first side as described in Steps 9 and 10, but use a long basting stitch. Remove the excess seam allowance and use it as a template to cut the second side, but do not stitch the second side after you cut it. Unstitch the first side to allow the garment to lie totally flat for embellishing. After you've completed your embellishment, stitch both sides and finish the seam allowances, starting at Step 12.

Mark the bust apex with safety pins to avoid undesirable embellishment or fabric focal point placement there.

11. Pin the seam allowance template along the second side of the sweatshirt. Cut along the inside edge of the template. If you will be embellishing over a shoulder, stop here and refer to the Design Note (above).

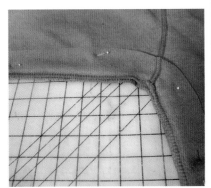
Pin the cut-off fabric from the first side onto the second side.

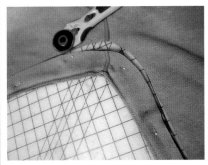
Cut away the excess material.

12. Pin the edges together and stitch, leaving a ⅜″ seam allowance. Clip the seam allowance of both underarm curves, clipping right up to the stitching but *not through it.*

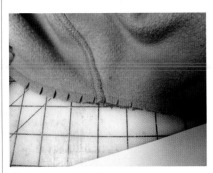
Clip both curved underarm seams.

tip

Clipping is necessary to keep the underarm area from puckering, pulling, and being stressed when the jacket is turned right side out.

13. Finish the seam allowances by using a serger or wide zigzag stitch to flatten the bulk, pulling the seams straight so that the underarm clips expand. It's okay for the needle to go off the fabric into the clipped spaces.

14. Determine a flattering length for the jacket at the front, sides, center back, and sleeves. Fold up and pin.

*A long jacket covering the hips often cuts the body in half and is **not** a flattering proportion, despite the common sentiment that concealing the hips will make one look thinner. Instead, try a shorter length, aiming for one-third of the ensemble's length from the jacket and two-thirds from the pants. Or go extra-long with the jacket so that the proportions are reversed: two-thirds for the jacket and one-third for the pants. (See Distinctive, page 83, to learn how to lengthen a jacket with fleece.)*

For a flattering, graceful hemline, make the center back at least ½″–1″ longer than the sides of the jacket. Avoid the finished sleeve length being even with the jacket hem when the arms are held at the sides. This creates a strong horizontal line that isn't flattering.

The Sweatshirt as Yardage

With this method of making and fitting a jacket, you cut the sweatshirt apart and use it as yardage. Individual pattern pieces are cut from the sweatshirt fabric, and the jacket is constructed using standard sewing methods, according to the specific project directions. You can use the patterns in this book or any basic pattern you've altered to fit your body, applying the neckline options for the book projects. Points to consider:

- Overall fit is improved using this method.

- The sleeve-to-body seam is raised to the natural shoulder line rather than remaining dropped.

- The need for a full-back alteration can be accommodated (for dowager's hump or rounded shoulders, for example).

- The front and back sections are cut as separate, flat pieces, so they are easier to embellish than an already-constructed garment.

- Generally with this method, you will want to consider lengthening the sleeves.

What Size?

Since you'll be using the sweatshirt as yardage and matching ribbing, you'll want to purchase a 2XL, or even 3XL (if available) for larger sizes, so that you'll have as much yardage as possible.

Size		Bust	Pattern bust measurement
S	6–8	32"–34" (81–86cm)	39⅞" (101cm)
M	10–12	35"–37" (89–94cm)	42⅞" (109cm)
L	14–16	38"–40" (97–102cm)	45⅞" (116cm)
XL	18–20	41"–43" (104–109cm)	48⅞" (124cm)
XXL	22–24	44"–46" (112–117cm)	51⅞" (131 cm)

Preparing the Pattern

Loose fitting is the industry term that describes the fit of the pattern pieces that are provided in the back pocket of this book. Determine the best size to use by measuring a garment that fits the way you like.

Seam allowances are ⅝" at the shoulders, sleeve to body, sides, and underarm sleeves. Neckline and center front seam allowances are ⅜".

Protect the original pattern by tracing the selected size onto tissue or pattern paper. Cut out the pattern pieces along the cutting lines and the appropriate neckline for the jacket you are creating. Mark ⅝" seamlines at the shoulders, sides, and sleeve underarms. Neckline and center front seam allowances are ⅜".

Fitting the Paper Pattern to You

1. Pin together the front and back pattern pieces along the shoulder seamlines, wrong sides together.

2. While wearing a top that you'll wear under the jacket and a good brassiere, try on the pattern—or fit the pattern onto a dress form if you have one. Pin the side seams the way you want your jacket to fit.

Pin the pattern to achieve the fit you want.

3. Now pin the underarm seams on the sleeve pattern and try it on, pinning to remove any excess from the front and/or back and matching the corresponding jacket body piece at the side seam. Pin the remaining sleeve underarm seam.

DESIGN NOTE

If you want your jacket sleeves to be longer than the sweatshirt fabric allows, include the additional length in your embellishment fabric allotment. Lengthen as described in the instructions for Sleeve Bands (page 21).

ALTERING THE JACKET FOR A FULL BACK

If you have extra body fullness at the back of the neck, you can adjust your jacket pattern accordingly. When the center back hemline swings out and up and the side seams swing to the back, as in the photograph (below), extra *length* is needed at the center back to accommodate the fullness in the back.

Slash along the pattern's back alteration line *between the armhole seamlines* to add length, gently pulling down on the pattern below the slash until the side seams hang straight. Fill in the cut pattern piece with tissue.

You will now need to add a shaped center back seam. Expand the pattern with tissue to create a ⅝" seam allowance at the center back.

Slash and spread the back to add length. Fill in the gap with pattern paper.

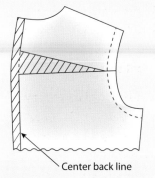

Center back line

Adding length and a center back seam solves the fit challenge.

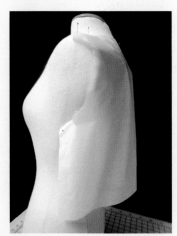

Backward and upward tilt shows that the back needs to be longer.

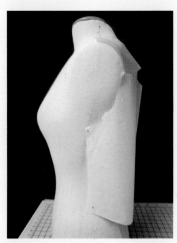

Much improved fit!

4. Now unpin your paper pattern pieces to get ready to cut out your fabric pieces.

tip

After you've created your jacket in fabric, pin any necessary fitting tuck or seam at the center back. Tweak the fit of the jacket to make it the absolute best fit for your body.

If needed, make a tuck or seam at the center back hemline.

Using the Sweatshirt Fabric

Follow the instructions for Preparing the Sweatshirt (page 8). Remove the sleeves by cutting on the sleeve side of the seam that joins them to the body of the sweatshirt. Cut the sleeves open along the underarm seam.

tip

The sleeves you cut from the original sweatshirt probably won't be identical in size. Don't worry—the pieces you cut from them will both be the same.

Cut along the side and shoulder seams to separate the front from the back. If there are no side seams, press the sweatshirt flat to establish the side seam locations and then cut along the pressed lines.

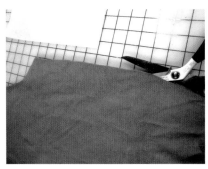

Cut apart along the side creases.

If a sweatshirt has seams on top of the shoulders, cut along those seams. If it has dropped front yoke seaming, leave the seams intact in case you need the extra length. You can cover them with embellishment.

Cutting and Marking

1. Fold the back and front pieces in half, wrong sides together, along a straight knit grainline (called a *course*). Do *not* be alarmed if all the edges don't line up. Lay out the pattern pieces for the jacket back and front on the available yardage. Pin in place, placing the pins at the bottom perpendicular to and extending *beyond* the pattern edge—a reminder *not* to cut the fabric there but to leave as much length as possible. Cut out the back and front pieces, cutting the bottom edge evenly at the longest point of the fabric available. Hemline curves or angles are flattering design options. Note the curve being cut in the photo.

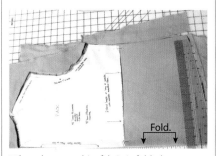

When the sweatshirt fabric is folded on the straight grain, the edges probably will *not* line up.

2. Place the 2 pieces of sleeve yardage wrong sides together, aligning the straight grains. Lay the sleeve pattern on the available sleeve yardage, pin in place, and cut out, making the sleeve as long as the fabric allows. Fold back the lower sleeve pattern piece to allow cutting a straight edge on the available fabric. Be sure to cut the front single notch and the back double notches *outward* as you cut your sleeve pieces.

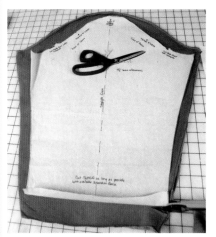

Fold back the pattern to cut a straight edge along the bottom edge of the sleeve.

DESIGN NOTE

Cutting on the grain is always preferred. But if length is more critical for your jacket than grain, just fold the sweatshirt yardage in half without worrying about grain and you'll undoubtedly end up with more length. Don't panic about the grain—no one will notice.

Size XXL note: *The pattern has been drafted with the average available fabric from an XXL sweatshirt. Regrettably, sweatshirt manufacturing is not standard, even within brands. Cut it as large as the fabric allows.*

3. Snip-mark a scant ¼″ into the seam allowance, perpendicular to the edge, at the dots along the armhole on the back, front, and sleeve fabric pieces.

Stabilizing the Neckline

These stabilizing steps apply to both Method 1 and Method 2 for the jacket construction. The back of the neckline might gap on your body, so it is vitally important to stabilize and shape it.

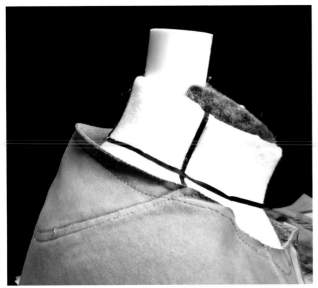

Before stabilizing, the back neckline stands out from the body.

1. Backstitch at one end of the back neckline; then stitch the neckline along the ⅜″ seamline, using polyester thread and a *long* stitch length. Leave long threads at the end of your stitching.

2. Pull the top thread to ease in the excess fabric at the neckline, pulling until the back edge hugs the neck snugly. Knot the thread ends to secure.

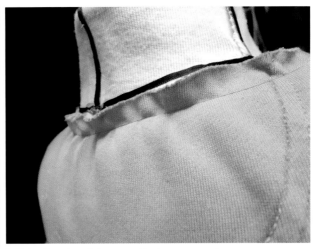

Pull the thread until the sweatshirt hugs your neck.

3. Lay the garment flat on an ironing surface, distribute the fullness equally, and steam shrink to remove the excess neck fullness. *Let the material cool before removing it from the ironing surface.*

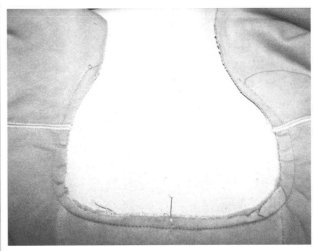

Steam to shrink the excess fullness in the neck.

 tip

Steam-shrinking extra fullness is possible only with a sweatshirt that is primarily cotton content.

Bias Strip Magic

Take the time to learn the following technique and you'll use it over and over again. This "magic" folding method yields long strips of perfect bias-grain strips without awkward cutting on the diagonal across large expanses of fabric—and it works on any shape, width, or length of fabric!

1. Using a single layer of fabric, fold down the upper left corner of your fabric piece at a 45° angle so that the left straight edge lies along the bottom straight edge.

Fold the upper left corner down to the bottom edge.

2. Fold the lower left point A up to the *new* folded point at the upper right point B (where there is a diagonal fold of 2 layers of fabric, not just a single layer). The fold you make at the left edge will lie on top of the original diagonal fold.

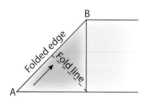

Fold the lower left point A up to the new point B at upper right.

3. Repeat the folding process, folding the new left point C to point B until your fabric tube is a convenient width for you to cut across.

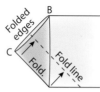

Keep folding until the fabric is an easy width to cut.

4. Fold any small remaining top point down onto the fabric tube.

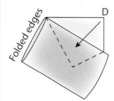

Fold down the final top point.

5. Align the left folded edge with vertical lines on your cutting mat. Set the straight edge rotary ruler in ¼″ or so over the left folded edges; cut off and discard these edges.

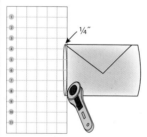

Cut off the folds on the left side.

6. Cut strips of the desired width across the fabric tube. After cutting the strips that you will use as banding, cut off the angled ends at 90°.

Trim the ends straight across.

7. If it is necessary to piece strips together, lay one bias strip end on top of another at a 90° angle, right sides together. Draw a diagonal line from the upper left to the lower right corner of the overlapped strips and stitch on the line. Trim the seam allowance to ¼″ and press open.

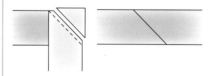

Lay bias strips right sides together at a right angle. Stitch on the diagonal. Trim and press.

Making Gathers

My technique for making gathering stitches takes advantage of a sewing machine's needle position capability. You stitch a line of gathering stitches on each side of what will be your stitched seam, pull the threads to gather the fabric, and then sew your seam between the two lines of stitching. Use strong polyester thread for this technique to prevent breakage.

Even if your machine doesn't have a positioning feature, this technique still works beautifully. Try it—you'll love it!

With Needle Position Adjustment

If your sewing machine allows you to adjust the position of the needle, follow these steps:

1. Place the fabric to be gathered, *wrong side up,* in position to sew with the seam allowance you want (⅝″, for example).

2. Move the needle position to stitch ⅛″ to the *left* of the eventual seam placement. Backstitch to start, and then sew long stitches the length of the seam; do not backstitch at the end. Leave long thread tails.

tip ....

Make your gathering stitches longer than normal but slightly shorter than basting stitches. You want them to be just long enough that you can easily pull up on the top thread to create gathers.

3. Move the needle position back to the center and then to the right to stitch ⅛″ to the *right* of the seamline. Backstitch, and then sew long stitches the length of the piece; do not backstitch at the end. Leave long thread tails.

4. With right sides together, match the gathered piece to the section it will join; pin at each end. Pull both of the top threads until the gathered piece is the same length as the base piece. Secure the thread ends by winding them in a figure 8 around the pin at the end.

Pull the gathering threads and wrap them around the last pin.

5. Distribute the gathers evenly across the piece. Stitch on the seamline *between* the 2 rows of gathering stitches, using a regular stitch length.

Stitch between the rows of gathering stitches.

6. Snip the backstitching of the first row of gathering stitches (the stitching on the garment side of the seam); pull out that thread completely. The bobbin thread will fall off on the outside of the gathered material.

Without Needle Position Adjustment

Here's what you do if your sewing machine *doesn't* have the needle position feature:

1. Position the fabric to be gathered, wrong side up, for the seam allowance width you want (⅝″, for example).

2. Move the fabric to the right to stitch ⅛″ to the *left* of the eventual seam placement. Backstitch to start, and then sew long stitches the length of the piece; do not back-stitch at the end. Leave long thread tails.

3. Now move the fabric to the left to stitch ¼″ to the *right* of the first row of gathering stitches. Backstitch, and then sew long stitches the length of the piece; do not back-stitch at the end. Leave long thread tails.

4. Repeat Steps 4–6 on page 17.

Setting Sleeves

1. On the wrong side of the sleeve, mark the ⅝″ armhole seamline with chalk. Pin the sleeve to the jacket body, right sides together, *only* at the following points:

- Underarm seams (forcing the body seam toward the back and the sleeve seam toward the front to balance the bulk)

- Shoulder (top notch of the sleeve to the shoulder seam of the body)

- Notches (single on front, double on back)

- Sleeve clips (those marking the dots above the sleeve notches to those marking the dots on the back and fronts)

The rest of the extra sleeve fabric will be eased in as you stitch.

Match the sleeve markings to the jacket body and pin in place.

2. With the inside of the sleeve facing up, stitch the sleeve to the jacket with the needle-down function engaged, if your machine has it. Operate the machine at a slow speed, using a stiletto (or some type of pointed tool, such as a Trolley Needle) to ease in the excess sleeve fabric between the notches and clips with *each* stitch. For 1″ at the very top of the sleeve, do not ease in any fabric.

Coax in the sleeve fullness with *every* stitch.

3. Double-stitch a bit toward the cut edge at the underarm between the notches. Trim the seam allowance to a shallower width at the underarm.

Double-stitch and trim at the underarm seam.

4. Finish the seam allowance by serging or using a wide zigzag stitch. Use a Chibi darning needle to tuck in the serger thread tail.

Finishing the Edges

Wrapped Band Finishing

A quick and easy way to finish the center front opening and the hem on your jacket body and sleeves, this technique can also be used to lengthen sleeves. The garment is cut to the *finished* size and length for wrapped band finishing.

> **DESIGN NOTE**
>
> *Bias-cut bands bend and turn more easily and lie flatter than straight-grain bands. And since a bias-finished outside edge won't ravel, you don't need to turn it under. Couched yarn or trim can be added to secure and conceal this raw edge, if you wish.*
>
> *Straight-grain bands are sometimes dictated by design or materials, but they are more successful on the center front than on sleeve and body hems. Bias bands work infinitely better for lower body edges. Any shaping at the lower hem will require cutting the band for a center back seam—and perhaps side seams. Wider bands require more seaming than narrow bands to accommodate hemline shaping.*

Band Sizes

BAND *WIDTH* FORMULA

1. To determine how wide to cut edge bands, decide how much fabric width you want to show on the *inside* of the jacket (this is the seam allowance) and multiply that by 2:

Desired inside width $\times$ 2 = A

2. Add ⅜″ for the "turn of cloth" edge thickness:

A + ⅜″ = B

3. Add the fabric width you want to show on the *outside* of the finished jacket:

B + Desired outside width = C

4. Add ¼″ for a turned-under edge on straight-grain bands (optional for bias bands):

C + ¼″ = D

D is the width to cut your band fabric.

> **DESIGN NOTE**
>
> *The ¼″ additional width figured into the front band size (D) allows for a turned-under finish. This extra ¼″ is optional for bias-grain bands, but it is advisable and useful for straight-grain edges. Whether you include it may also be determined by the width of the yarn or trim you use for embellishment couching—how well the yarn can encase and cover the interior edge if you don't want a "furry" raw bias edge as a finish.*

BAND *LENGTH* FORMULA

Lower edge and neck bands: Refer to the individual project instructions.

Center front bands: Cut 3″ longer than the finished length.

Sleeve bands: Cut 2″ longer than the finished circumference at the sleeve edge.

> **DESIGN NOTE**
>
> *If your sleeve band or front band fabric is a directional print, cut the bands so they are mirror images of each other. Mark the neckline and hemline of each band to prevent confusion. If the fabric is reversible, be sure to mark the right side of each to prevent mistakes.*

Cut mirror-image bands from a directional print.

Attaching the Bands

JACKET HEMLINE BANDS

Attach hemline bands before attaching center front bands. Techniques to use follow Steps 1–3 and 5–9 under Center Front Bands (below), utilizing one long band the length of the cut hemline. Consult specific project instructions for more information.

CENTER FRONT BANDS

1. Stabilize the garment front edges by fusing Straight Fusible Stay Tape along the raw edges of the center front pieces on the *right* side of the fabric.

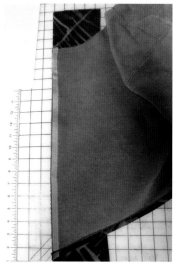

Fuse on stay tape and position the band along the front edge.

2. Cut 2 front bands, following the center front Band Width and Band Length Formulas (page 19). Position the band to extend ¾″ lower than the bottom edge of the jacket front, with the rest of the excess length at the neckline. Pin the *right* side of the band to the *wrong* side of the garment, aligning the long edges.

---

tip

The quilting guide hiding in many machine accessory boxes is very helpful for stitching seams that are wider than the measurements designated by the throat plate markings. A walking foot for your machine will be helpful in stitching these bulky, layered seams.

3. Stitch the bands to each side of the jacket front, using the seam allowance determined in Step 1 of the Band Width Formula (page 19). Use an acrylic ruler and rotary cutter to trim the cut edge *just a tad* so that the seam allowance is *exactly* even.

4. From the inside of the jacket, press the band outward, away from the jacket. Press the excess band length at the lower edge up, flush with the finished hemline band.

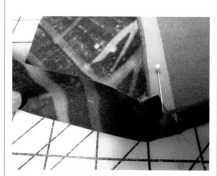

For a neat finish, first fold up the band's extra hem length at the bottom.

5. Now fold the bottom edge of each band into place on the right side of the jacket, making the folds even with the hemline. Pin along the folded edge of the bands.

---

6. Accurately measure the band width that you want to show on the jacket front from Step 3 of the Band Width Formula (page 19), plus the optional ¼″ turn-under if you added it in Step 4 of the formula. Fold this to the outside of the jacket front and pin in place. Turn under the optional ¼″ if you added it. Press.

The front bands fold over *after* the extra length is turned up.

7. Zigzag stitch the turned-under or raw edge to the jacket front, using monofilament thread in the needle (0.5 to 1 wide and 3 long are the stitch settings on my machine).

8. Refer to Couching Basics (page 24) to embellish the inner edge of the band with couched yarn according to your design plan, and burying the yarn. Then slipstitch the bottom folded edge by hand.

9. At the neckline edge, trim the excess length of the front bands to align with the jacket edge. This raw edge will be finished off with the neckline treatments in the individual projects.

10. Steam press to improve the look of everything!

SLEEVE BANDS

1. Stabilize the sleeve hem by fusing Straight Fusible Stay Tape along the edge on the *right* side of the sleeve.

2. Cut 2 sleeve bands, following the Band Width and Band Length Formulas (page 19).

DESIGN NOTE

If the sleeves need to be longer, cut band widths twice the desired additional sleeve length plus 1" (for the seam allowance and finishing). Refer to jacket directions for Adorned *and* Innovative *for specific directions. Interface the half of the band width that will flip up to show on the outside of the extended sleeve (see photo, page 31).*

3. With the *right* side of the band (the half that's not interfaced if you are lengthening the sleeves) facing the *wrong* side of the sleeve, begin pinning at the sleeve seam, turning back approximately ¾" at the starting end of the band and placing this fold flush with the sleeve seamline.

4. Using the machine's free arm, stitch the band to the sleeve using the previously determined seam allowance from Step 1 in Band Width Formula (page 19). When you stitch back to your starting point, overlap the folded-back beginning edge with the remaining fabric and stitch to secure.

Fold back the starting end and stitch around the sleeve, overlapping the band ends.

5. Use an acrylic ruler and rotary cutter to trim the seam allowance so it is *exactly* even by trimming the cut edge of the seam just a tad. Press and turn the band to the outside of the sleeve. For sleeve-lengthening bands, press up the interfaced half of the band, letting the seam allowance extend down toward the band.

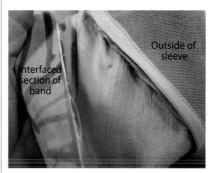

With the seam allowance forced down, the interfaced portion is folded to the outside.

ADDING A HIDDEN FRONT CLOSURE

For an invisible yet secure closure for the jacket's front bands, use this "hanging" snap technique.

Stitch the male side of a jumbo snap completely out of sight on the back-side of one center front band. Stitch the female side of the snap to the opposite band so that it hangs out partway from the inside, as shown in the photo below. The two edges will butt together when the snap is fastened.

A hanging snap closure is invisible and secure.

6. Accurately measure the band width that you want to show on the outside of the sleeve from Step 3 of Band Width Formula (page 19), plus the optional ¼″ turn-under if you added it in Step 4 of the formula. Fold this to the outside of the sleeve and pin the band in place. Turn under the optional ¼″ edge at the top if you added it. For bands used to lengthen sleeves, turn under the allotted ½″. Stitch the sleeve band in place along the folded edge.

7. Embellish with couched yarn according to your design plan, leaving 7″ tails of yarn as you begin and end your stitching. Bury the tails between fabric layers, using a Chibi darning needle, as directed in Couching Basics (page 24).

8. On the outside of the sleeve or band extension, hand slipstitch the vertical folded band end at the underarm seam.

Twin-Needle Hemming

If you prefer a turned-under hem on your jacket, use a cover hem machine or a serger with a cover hem stitch, if that option is available to you. Otherwise, discover the twin needle capability on your sewing machine. Any machine that's threaded from front to back can use twin needles! *The secret to success is using Knit Fusible Stay Tape to eliminate ripply "roller coaster" hemlines. This is a great* hem technique for any and all knits!

1. Turn up the hem as desired and press. Do not trim the hem allowance to an even depth at this point. Measure and compare to make sure the sides and the center fronts are the same length—or not, if that's your design.

2. Clip the seam allowance of the side seams at the pressed hemline. Above the hemline, press the seam allowance toward the garment back. Within the hem allowance, press the seam allowance toward the front.

3. Fuse Knit Fusible Stay Tape to the inside of the *hem allowance* along the stitching line for your hem as shown. In Step 5 you will be sewing through the tape with twin needle stitching.

Clip and press the seam allowance and then fuse the stay tape.

4. Using a 4.0/75 twin stretch needle, thread your machine top thread with either 2 spools or 2 filled bobbins, not one of each. If the thread source rides horizontally, also use identical spool caps. Make sure the threads wind off their sources in opposite directions—the way the threads feed affects the tension and thus the stitching.

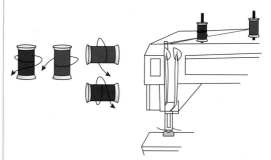

Make sure the threads wind off in opposing directions.

tip

Experiment to determine if your machine works best with the threads on opposite sides of the upper tension disc, or with both threads on one side or the other. Machines—and experts—differ on this point. Decreasing the upper thread tension might further improve the stitching.

5. Set the stitch length at approximately 7 stitches per inch. Stitch the hem with the right side of the garment facing up; the bobbin thread zigzags on the inside of the garment, creating a stretchy hemline. Use a quilting guide, a seam guide, or even a sticky note appropriately placed on the machine bed to help you keep your stitching straight and even. Leave long threads at both ends of your stitching—do not backstitch when using twin needles.

Stitch the jacket hem.

6. Using duckbill appliqué scissors, *carefully* trim away the extra hem allowance above the stitching.

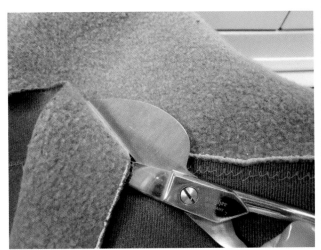

Trim away the excess hem allowance.

tip

Duckbill appliqué scissors are helpful, but they won't totally prevent you from cutting into the outer garment—so take care!

Fabric "Fur" Trim

Everything from rich hand-woven fabrics to inexpensive polyester crepe, menswear suits and ties, home-decorating silks and tapestries, wool crepe, and silk dupioni (my favorite) makes excellent "fur" trim when cut on the bias and roughed up with a stiff Fabric Chenille Brush—and all without washing! Even denim works to create great fabric fur, although denim must be laundered to really work. Especially wonderful are iridescent fabrics with different-colored yarns running in the warp (lengthwise) and weft (crosswise). Fabrics that *don't* work well are high-thread-count, tightly woven fabrics (batiks) and printed quilting cottons that have a pale white wrong side.

Always test to make sure you like the look before you cut lots of strips! Strips can be a variety of colors, but be sure the color of the top layer contrasts with the (optional) center couched yarn. Your strips can be equal or different widths, though I find that if the fabric frays well, cutting different widths isn't worth the trouble.

Making the "Fur"

1. Cut bias strips approximately ¼″ wider than your desired finished trim width (see Bias Strip Magic, page 16); 3 to 5 layers work well.

> **tip**
>
> Cut off any selvage ends from your strips—the selvages won't ravel for fur trim.

2. Layer the strips and stitch down the center. Use the needle-down function on the sewing machine, if available, to hold everything in place as you add layers of strips. If you need longer strips, just lap and pin on more strips as necessary.

Layer and stitch the bias strips, pinning on more strips to add length.

3. Use your rotary cutter and ruler to trim the strip layers to an equal width on each side of the center stitching to achieve the trim size desired.

4. Now attack the strips with your Fabric Chenille Brush! Brush in both directions and from both front and back sides.

5. Attach the fur trim to the project, and then couch contrasting-colored yarn down the center of the bias trim (see Couching Basics, below).

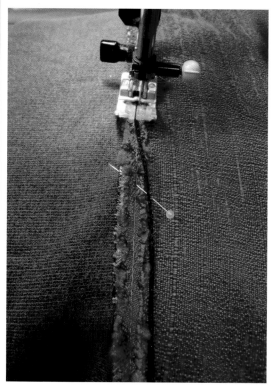

Black yarn being couched down center

Couching Basics

Couching is a method of attaching yarn or narrow trim using a zigzag stitch.

The best trim enhances or contrasts with the base garment. Look for yarns that have a bit of character or texture. Consider twisting different yarns together for the perfect color solution. For hand-woven fabrics, a pulled yarn of the fabric itself can provide the perfect "yarn" for couching. Avoid hand-dyed spotty-colored yarns and yarns with vastly differing character along their length.

1. Thread your machine with monofilament thread on top (clear for light colors, smoke for dark colors) and regular polyester thread in the bobbin (matching the garment fabric).

2. Test the machine's upper tension, using a zigzag stitch set just wide enough to encompass your trim and a stitch length that's a little longer than normal, to accommodate the sweatshirt thickness. If dots of the bobbin thread show at the tip of each zigzag stitch, you need to *loosen* the upper tension by making the appropriate adjustment for your machine. On my machine I adjust the tension to a lower number.

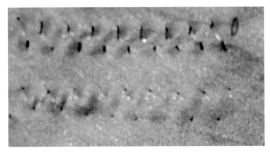

The top row shows unbalanced tension—the bobbin thread is peeking out at the points of the zigzag stitch. Remedy the problem by loosening the upper tension (bottom row).

3. Lay your trim evenly on the base to which you're sewing it, leaving a 7˝ tail at each end. Zigzag stitch in place, taking care *not to pull the trim or stretch the base* as you work.

Couched yarn trim

Hold the twisted yarns in place with a Trolley Needle.

4. Thread the yarn tail on a Chibi darning needle; then poke the needle back between the layers and out on the wrong side of the jacket. Clip the yarn end close to the jacket. This is better and more secure than knotting the yarn.

Use a Chibi darning needle to bury the yarn ends.

Adorned

Designed and made by Londa Rohlfing

Materials

- Basic Supplies (page 7)

- Sweatshirt (size 2XL),
80% cotton / 20% polyester

- 1½ yards fabric (44″ wide) for
cuffs, bands, lining, and bias-strip
embellishment

- 10 yards yarns or trims for
embellishment

- ⅜ yard interfacing for cuffs,
if you lengthen the sleeves

- 4 yards Straight Fusible Stay Tape

- 3 yards fusible web ½″ wide

DESIGN NOTE

*When considering companion
fabrics for your sweatshirt, look
at both sides of the material. For
this jacket I used the wrong side
of the batik fabric as my right
side for a softer look.*

Getting Started

Because this jacket is fitted with
Method 2 (page 12), use pattern
pieces 1, 2, 3, and 6. Follow the
steps for Preparing the Sweatshirt
(page 8). Fit and cut the jacket
pieces according to Method 2
(page 12), following the neckline
designated on pattern tissue
piece 6 for this design. Be sure to
machine baste only the side and
shoulder seams when checking
the fit.

Follow the directions for Stabilizing
the Neckline (page 15).

Embellishing with Couching

For general guidelines for applying
yarn embellishment, refer to
Couching Basics (page 24).

1. Remove the shoulder and side
seam basting from the fitting process to make it easier to embellish
the front and back pieces.

2. Stabilize the jacket front center
edges with Straight Fusible Stay
Tape as shown. Then use chalk
to mark major horizontal and
diagonal directional lines, approximately 1″ apart, for the couched
embellishment.

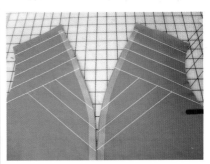

Mark horizontal and diagonal lines
for couching.

tip

The horizontal embellishment area
on the front, with couching lines
running parallel to the shoulder
seam, extends down 4¼″ from the
shoulder seamline. The diagonal
embellishment section angles
up from the bust level at the
center front to intersect with the
horizontal section 1½″ from the
armhole seam.

3. Press and fold to mark the center back. Mark your couching design on the upper third of the back. The back length of the sample jacket is 24″, and the embellishment covers the upper 8″. Your jacket length may vary from this length, but the idea is that you embellish the top one-third of your jacket length.

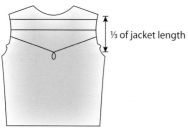

⅓ of jacket length

Mark the embellishment lines. Make the embellished area no more than one-third of the jacket length.

DESIGN NOTE

Avoid visually dividing an area into two equal sections with your embellishment—unequal proportions are more pleasing to the eye.

4. On both the front and back sections, add a few main lines of couching using a dominant yarn or trim, or any trim that you have in limited supply, reserving enough for the sleeves. When stitching symmetrically designed front sections, it is easiest to stitch directly from one side to the other. Then cut trim between the 2 fabric pieces. Leave a ⅝″ gap between the horizontal and diagonal couched sections for a folded bias strip of fabric. This strip will visually connect the front of the jacket and the neckline banding.

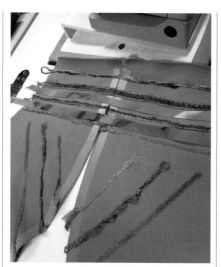

Couch several major design lines, stitching from one section to another.

DESIGN NOTE

As you assess your yarns or trims, you'll need to decide two things:

■ How solid do you want the couched areas to be—how much of the sweatshirt fabric do you want to be visible?

■ Do you prefer symmetrical or asymmetrical balance? Will each side exactly mirror the other, with trims placed in exactly the same order (symmetrical), or will the two sides be different? The jacket in the photographs features symmetrical embellishment.

There is no right or wrong choice—it's whatever you like. You are the designer!

5. Have fun with your couching! Consider twisting ribbon-type trim, for instance, or try stitching some yarns on top of narrow bias fabric strips. Finish couching the front and the back sections. The back has a straight back center line of embellishment over the diagonal lines of couching. Then the bottom row of couching has a center loop of embellishment for added interest on the back. Refer to the photo (page 29) for the detail.

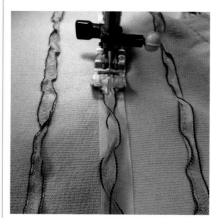

Play with couching to get the effect you want.

Completed couching leaving a ⅝″ open space for a folded bias fabric strip.

Adding Bias Strips

1. Following the Bias Strip Magic instructions (page 16), cut bias fabric strips 2¼˝ wide and long enough to span the yoke where they will be placed on the front and back sections. Press in half lengthwise, *wrong* sides together.

2. Position each front yoke strip along the bottom of the space between the horizontal and diagonal couching, with the fold toward the shoulder. Stitch ⅜˝ from the raw edge.

Stitch the folded bias strip in place.

3. Flip the folded edge of the bias strip down, concealing the raw edges of the seam allowance. Couch yarn along the stitched top edge, leaving the bottom fold loose.

4. In the same way, attach the bias strip to the back along the bottom of the horizontal embellished area. Fold down and couch as in Step 3.

Back bias strip

Cutting and Attaching the Lining

1. Use the embellished jacket sections as the patterns to cut lining pieces large enough to conceal the embellishment stitching on the inside of the jacket. Cut the bottom edge of the lining sections ½˝ longer than the embellished section of each yoke. As you cut the neckline and armholes, lay the *wrong* side of the embellished pieces against the *wrong* side of the lining.

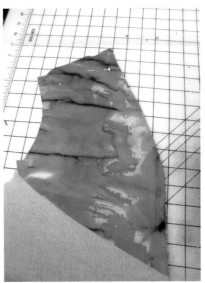

Cut the bodice yoke linings.

2. Turn under the bottom edges of the lining ½˝ and attach to the jacket using strips of fusible web along the edges of the yoked area to secure the lining in place. Stitch to attach at the neckline, shoulder seams, and armholes.

Turn under the bottom edge and fuse to attach.

Assembling the Jacket

1. Using a ⅝˝ seam, stitch the shoulder seams, easing the back shoulder seam into the front shoulder seam. The lining will help to stabilize the front shoulder seams.

tip

Except when you are inserting sleeves, always orient the piece to be eased toward the feed dogs at the sewing machine. The feed dogs will automatically work in excess fullness.

2. Trim the back shoulder seam allowance to stagger or "grade" the fabric layers by trimming the seam allowance to ⅜˝ and the front seam allowance to ½˝. This will eliminate some of the bulk in the seam area. Then finish off the front edge of the seam allowance by serging or stitching with a large, wide zigzag.

3. Press the finished seam allowance toward the back. Invisibly topstitch from the outside using monofilament thread on top to secure the seam allowance.

4. Double-check the fit of the jacket. Stitch and finish the side seams. Press the seam allowances toward the back.

5. Stitch and finish the seams of each sleeve. Press toward the front of the sleeves.

6. Insert the sleeves into the body and stitch, following the directions for Setting Sleeves (page 18). Only by attaching the sleeves can you determine a flattering length for both the sleeves and the body of the jacket.

Finishing the Edges

DESIGN NOTE

The bias band finish for the jacket hem doesn't need to be the same width as the center front / neckline edging. The jacket in the photographs uses a narrower, less-attention-getting width for the hem and a wider center front band that creates a strong, figure-flattering vertical. A twin-needle (page 22) or cover-stitched hem (available on some sergers) would be a flattering finish for larger body sizes, downplaying attention at the hipline. Do what is most attractive for your body.

Directions follow for a narrow body hem banding. If you want a twin-needle hem instead, do that now. Always finish horizontal edges before vertical edges.

Jacket Hem

1. Fit the jacket to establish an attractive finished hem length and shaping. The lower back hem on this jacket comes to a point. You determine your own hem shape for the back. Refer to the photo (below) for this detail.

2. Refer to Bias Strip Magic (page 16) to cut enough bias strips to finish the lower edge of your jacket, following the Band Width and Band Length Formulas (page 19). You determine the band width that you desire to show on the hem of your jacket.

3. Add the bottom finishing band, following the directions for Wrapped Band Finishing (page 19). Stabilize the hemline edge, using Straight Fusible Stay Tape. If you have designed your hemline with a point in the back, miter to fold in any excess hem allowance at the center back.

Lower back hem

4. Couch trim to finish the band, if desired.

Consider twisting 2 yarns to finish the hem band.

5. Trim the ends of the hem band flush with the center front edges.

Center Front and Neckline

1. Before proceeding with these steps, refer to Center Front Bands (page 20). Cut, position, and attach the center front bands as directed for Wrapped Band Finishing (page 19), noting the following:

■ Measure your jacket and cut a 2½″-wide bias band long enough to span the center front and neckline edge plus 2″. Take care that any seaming falls at the back neckline.

■ Pin the right side of the band to the wrong side of the jacket with ¾″ of the band extending beyond the bottom edges of the jacket. Stitch using a ⅝″ seam, easing in extra band length at the back neckline as you stitch. Easing extra band length at the back neckline is very important when using a band this wide. Trim the seam allowance to ½″.

2. Twist and couch yarn to finish the inner band edge, leaving 6″ tails at both ends. Bury the yarn tails as described in Couching Basics (page 24).

Sleeve Hem

Cut the sleeve bands following the Band Width and Band Length Formulas (page 19). Bias bands are best. If you need to lengthen the sleeves, an interfaced bias band (page 21) is necessary. You can interface either the entire sleeve band width or just the half that will be the "outer" band. This band can be cut either twice as wide as desired (plus 1″ for seaming to the sleeve and finishing) if there is a fold at the lowermost edge, or into 4 sleeve bands, allowing for a lowermost seam that joins the outer (interfaced) bands to the inner bands. The seam allowance of joining the inner band to the sleeve itself (right side inner band to wrong side sleeve) should be allowed to extend toward the sleeve band. Refer to Sleeve Bands (page 21) to stabilize and add the finishing bands to the sleeves. Add couching to the sleeve bands as desired.

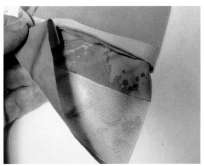

Seam allowance extends toward the sleeve band.

Carefree

Designed and made by Londa Rohlfing

SKILL LEVEL: *Easy*

FITTING: *Method 1*

Materials

- Basic Supplies (page 7)

- Sweatshirt with hood and front zipper (close to natural size)

- 1¼ yards fabric (45″ wide) for hood lining and trim

- 1 yard Straight Fusible Stay Tape

- Yarn for embellishment

- Needle wheel (*optional*)

- Pinking shears (*optional*)

Getting Started

This project does not use any of the tissue pattern pieces because Method 1 is used for the fitting.

1. Follow the steps for Preparing the Sweatshirt (page 8). Ample sleeve length is assumed so that the sleeve ribbing can be removed.

2. Use Method 1 (page 9) for this jacket. If you want a closer fit in the jacket body or sleeves, follow the instructions for Shaping the Sweatshirt (page 9). Make sure that the sleeve circumference is the same for the last 7″ of the lower sleeve.

3. Pull the hood cord so that it is equally extended on both sides at the center front. Stitch through *all* the layers at the center back to anchor the cord.

Stitch through the hood casing in back to anchor the drawstring cord.

Lining the Hood

> *tip*
>
> The hood lining is cut on the bias rather than the straight grain because it actually folds and turns, and it will do that more readily when cut on the bias.

1. Turn the hood inside out, fold it in half with the center back seam to the left, and place it over pattern tissue. Trace the outermost edges of the hood: center back neckline edge, over the top curve, to the front edge. Keep the hood in place on the pattern tissue.

2. With the hood still on the pattern tissue, use a pin or a needle wheel to mark the neck edge on the tissue, stabbing through all layers along the *bottom edge* of the neck banding to create perforations in the tissue. This perforated "line" in the tissue becomes the seamline. *Add* a ⅝″ seam allowance to this perforated seamline to provide a nice finished edge at the neckline.

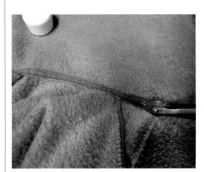

Mark the edge where the hood attaches to the jacket, using a needle wheel or stabbing repeatedly with a pin.

3. On the pattern, draw a straight-grain line parallel to the center back edge of the hood.

4. Establish the bias-grain line by folding the pattern tissue at a 45° angle to the marked bottom neckline edge of the hood; crease. Mark the diagonal folded line as the grainline, which is now bias. By cutting the lining on the bias grain, the lining will conform to the hood more easily.

5. Add a ¼″ seam allowance to the hood lining pattern along the center back and top. Cut out the paper pattern.

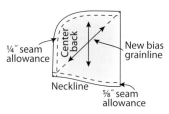

The hood lining pattern shows perforations for bottom edge, straight-grain line, 45° bias-grain line, and ¼″ seam allowance on curved center back/top edge.

6. Align the marked bias-grain line of the pattern with the straight grain of 2 layers of the lining fabric, right sides of fabric together, and cut out the hood lining.

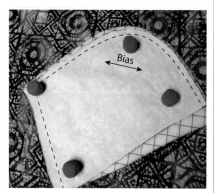

Cut the hood lining from doubled fabric.

7. With right sides together, stitch the lining pieces together along the continuous center back and top seamline, using a ¼″ seam allowance. Press flat as stitched to "seal" the seam.

8. Trim the curve with pinking shears to automatically notch the excess seam allowance. Alternatively, you can cut notches (though not as many) with scissors to eliminate bulk in the seam along the curve when it is turned.

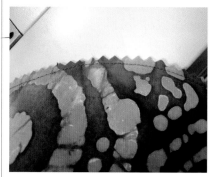

Pinking shears automatically notch the curve.

9. With wrong sides together, align the raw front edge of the lining fabric with the outside folded edge of the hood. Align the center lining seam with the hood's center seam and pin the lining to the hood all along the back center seam of the hood.

Pin the lining seam to the back center seam of the hood.

10. At the neckline and outer front hood edges, turn under the raw edges and pin the lining, clipping if necessary, so that it lies smoothly.

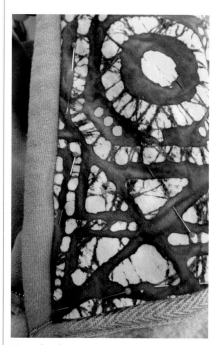

Pin under the raw edges at the neckline and front of the hood.

tip

I had to actually release the center back seam a bit at the neck edge for this edge to lie nicely against the jacket.

11. Turn the pins perpendicular to the seam along the center back and top.

12. With the lining facing up and your machine threaded with mono-filament thread on top and regular thread (matching the sweatshirt) in the bobbin, stitch in-the-ditch of the center back hood seam with a straight stitch to securely connect the lining to the hood.

Stitch on the seam to attach the lining to the sweatshirt hood.

13. With the lining side up, use a narrow zigzag stitch (1.5 stitch width, 3 stitch length on my machine) to sew around the neckline and outer front hood edge, taking care to keep the hood tie ends loose at the center front edges.

Attach the neck and front lining edges with zigzag stitching.

Hood lining securely attached to the sweatshirt

Banding the Pockets

1. If you have thread that perfectly matches the outer stitching on the sweatshirt, carefully rip out both ends of the pockets so that they are free for at least 1½˝.

If you don't have a perfect thread match, *remove the pockets completely*—you'll sew them back on after the edges are bound and embellished.

2. Cut out and apply fabric bandings to the front pouch pocket edges, following the steps for Wrapped Band Finishing (page 19). Cut the bandings 3˝ wide and 2˝ longer than the pocket edge.

Band the edges of the front pouch pockets.

3. Trim both ends of the banding to ½˝ and turn under so they line up with the original pocket shape.

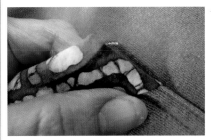

Turn the ends under flush with the pocket edges.

4. Couch yarn along the interior trim edge, referring to Couching Basics (page 24).

5. Pin the bound pocket edge back into place on the jacket. Leaving long threads at both ends, stitch to connect to the original sweatshirt stitching, sewing around the corner and back to the other side. (You'll be stitching 3 sides of a rectangle.) Bury the thread ends as directed in Couching Basics (page 24). If you completely removed the pockets, reattach them now, following the original stitching lines.

Restitch the bound pocket edge to the sweatshirt.

Banding the Hem Ribbing

tip

The ribbing along the bottom edge of the jacket *must* remain intact because the zipper is attached to it.

Cut and attach the hemline band according to the directions for Wrapped Band Finishing (page 19), making the following adjustments:

1. Refer to Bias Strip Magic (page 16) to cut bias banding 2 times the width of the lower ribbing *plus* ⅞˝, and the length of the lower ribbing *plus* 2˝, piecing if necessary at the center back. This allows for a ¼˝ seam allowance, ⅜˝ for the "turn of cloth," and ¼˝ to turn under at the finished edge on the outside.

2. Lay the right side of the banding against the wrong side of the sweatshirt, with the banding extending ¼˝ over the seamline; leave 1˝ of the banding extending past each center front edge. Stitch with a ¼˝ seam allowance. Trim the excess at each end to ½˝ and turn back the excess length from the center front edges as shown.

On the wrong side of the sweatshirt, attach the banding with a ¼˝ seam allowance.

Trim and turn back the extra banding at both ends.

3. Wrap the banding to the outside and pin in place. Turn under the upper banding edge and cover it with couched yarn, leaving 7˝ yarn tails at both ends. Bury the yarn ends with a Chibi darning needle, as directed in Couching Basics (page 24).

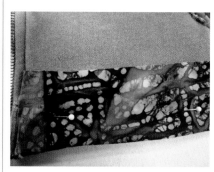

Pin the banding in place on the outside of the jacket.

Couch yarn to attach the banding edge, leaving 7˝ yarn ends.

Adding Hood Trim

1. On the *inside* of the hood, couch yarn along the fabric edge from one side of the neck to the other, being careful to keep the tie cord free and leaving 7″ of yarn at each end.

Couch yarn on the inside where the fabric meets the sweatshirt.

2. Bury the ends of the yarn with a Chibi darning needle, as directed in Couching Basics (page 24).

Bury the yarn ends to finish the trim.

tip

Only if your machine uses a *metal* bobbin, wind monofilament thread onto the metal bobbin for Step 3 to make the stitching invisible on the inside zipper edge of the jacket. Otherwise, bobbin thread that matches the sweatshirt will work fine.

3. Couch yarn along the center front and outside hood edges, starting at one hem edge, continuing around the hood, and ending at the other hem edge. Bury the yarn ends at the hemline with a Chibi darning needle.

Couch yarn on both sides of the zipper and around the outer stitching line on the hood.

Making the Adjustable Cuffs

The sleeve band is extra-wide because it rolls to the outside to become a cuff. (On the sample jacket, *the Step 1 width using the Band Width Formula, page 19, was 3″!*) Embellishment is not necessary, as the edge will be covered when the cuff rolls back to the outside of the sleeve.

DESIGN NOTE

Only bias-cut fabric will work for this extra-deep sleeve cuff that turns back on itself. This is a great finish for easy sleeve length adjustment—perfect for jackets you are making as gifts or to sell.

1. Decide on the finished sleeve length you want and determine how much length is available to roll back to the outside.

The cuff at the left isn't turned; the sleeve at the right shows the turned-back cuff.

2. Follow the directions for Wrapped Band Finishing (page 19) to attach the sleeve bands, being sure to allow for an extra-wide band measurement and to stabilize the sleeve edges with Straight Fusible Stay Tape.

Amplified

Designed and made by Londa Rohlfing

Materials

- Basic Supplies (page 7)

- Sweatshirt (sized according to the fitting method you use), 80% cotton / 20% polyester

- ¾ yard *each* of 3 coordinating fabrics (2 positive/negative prints for shoulder/back embellishment and 1 coordinating stripe for bias bands)

- 1 large button, approximately 1½˝ diameter

- Elastic ponytail band (in a color to go with the jacket)

- Yarns for embellishment, 1 "quiet" and 1 "loud" (a black-and-silver "quiet" yarn and a hairy red and black "loud" yarn were used for sample jacket)

- 2¼–3 yards trim (2¼ yards snap tape were used for sample jacket in size medium)

- ⅜˝ Clover Bias Tape Maker

- 1 yard lightweight fusible web (such as Mistyfuse)

- 4 yards Straight Fusible Stay Tape

Getting Started

Follow the steps for Preparing the Sweatshirt (page 8). Be sure to *retain the sweatshirt's bottom ribbing* for use as the neckline finish.

Fit and construct the jacket according to whichever technique you prefer. Method 1 (page 9) was used for the sample jacket. If you use Method 2 (page 12) to make your jacket, you will use pattern pieces 1, 2, and 3.

The jacket offers some design options. Here are some suggestions you might want to use in the design of your jacket:

- Add a pocket created from a mix of 2 coordinating fabrics at the lower left front.

- Design the back angle from the left back shoulder down to the lower right hemline with pieced fabrics peeking over the left front shoulder.

- Shape and cut the front hemlines as you wish (see the Design Note, page 40). The hemline cut edge equals the finished body length that will be bound.

Design and press the hem; then cut to the finished length.

The jacket in the photos demonstrates asymmetrical or informal balance, since the two sides are different—on purpose. The front hem is rounded on one side and angled on the other. This jacket was purposely designed with informal balance to offer creative opportunities. For a symmetrically balanced hem, simply make both front hemlines either rounded or angled. Make your jacket yours! Directions follow for the sample jacket—adapt them as you wish.

Designing the Jacket Body

1. On the fronts, follow the neckline designated on the pattern tissue for this jacket. Refer to Stabilizing the Neckline (page 15). Staystitch the neckline ⅜˝ from the edge. Fit and control the neckline by pulling up a thread of the stay stitching so that the neckline hugs the neck; knot off the threads. Steam to shrink out the fullness; let cool.

2. On a dress form or with a helper, with the sweatshirt *right side out,* mark a straight diagonal slash in the back. The sample jacket slash extends from the lower left hemline to the upper right shoulder.

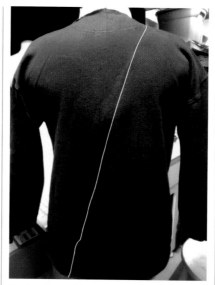

Mark a diagonal slash on the jacket back.

3. Cut the slash mark and lap one side of the back slash over the other side, pinning to fit as desired.

4. Decide on the size of the back area to be embellished with pieced fabrics. The area to the right of the slash is marked for embellishment. Mark the lowermost opposite edge of this area on the right jacket back.

Pin the back slash to fit. The area to the right of the slash is to be embellished with fabric.

5. With the jacket lying flat, use pins to mark the "lap to" line on the left side of the back where the cut edge ends. Unpin the right side along the back slash. Apply Straight Fusible Stay Tape to the left back so that the left edge of the tape runs along the "lap to" line.

Fuse stay tape to the right of the "lap to" line on the left back.

6. Pin the right slashed edge back into place and stitch with a large, wide zigzag stitch (3 long and 4.5 wide on my machine) through all the layers of the jacket back, stitching ¼˝ from the cut edge and through the stay tape.

Zigzag stitch the right slash edge over the stay tape.

7. Decide on the finished back hem length and mark the desired length at the side seams and in back. (Keep the trim you've selected in mind: if it's a straight-grain trim, don't design a really curvy hemline.) Trim the excess hem length to create a clean-cut finished length edge for the entire bottom edge.

Design and cut the back hemline.

8. Stabilize the entire hemline edge by applying Straight Fusible Stay Tape right along the cut edge on the *outside* of the jacket.

Designing the Fabric Sections

1. Refer to the photos of the front and back of the jacket (page 40) for design ideas. Lay tissue over the jacket on the front and back areas to be embellished with pieced fabric. Trace the large, overall shape you desire. Try sketching to determine the number and shape of sections that will look good. An odd number of areas creates a better design. With a piece of chalk, mark the outermost lines of the embellished area onto the sweatshirt. Label the tissue to assign fabrics to each section.

Visually connect the sections between front and back at the very top of the shoulder line on the right front, not at the dropped-front yoke shoulder line (assuming you are using Method 1). Trim will be added on top of the shoulder where the front and back fabric sections join, so they don't need to intersect perfectly.

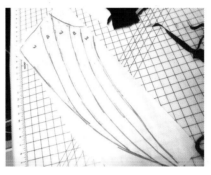

Fabric section design for sample jacket back

2. After sketching your final fabric section shapes, lay tissue over them and trace each section. Label to designate the order of the pieces and the fabric you want to use for each one. Cut apart.

Trace the fabric section shapes on tissue and label each section.

3. Remembering that fabric cut on the bias will bend and drape better than straight-grain fabric, cut your shapes from fabric as desired, cutting each piece ¼" larger than the tissue pattern on all sides. Apply fusible web to the back of each fabric section, if desired.

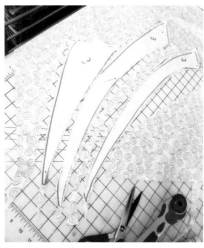

Cut on the bias, adding ¼" all around.

Attaching the Fabric Sections

Lay the fabric sections on the sweatshirt as desired, lapping the edges of the dark colors over the light colors. Pin to secure and zigzag stitch the pieces to the sweatshirt, using monofilament thread in the needle (1.5 wide and 3 long on my machine).

Cover and embellish the edges of the fabric sections, using one of the following techniques.

Sample Jacket Embellishment

1. Create narrow fusible bias banding by using the Clover ⅜" Fusible Bias Tape Maker, following the manufacturer's instructions.

Clover Fusible Bias Tape Maker

2. Fuse bias tape between each fabric section to cover the edges. Secure with straight stitching down each side of the bias tape, using monofilament thread as the top thread.

3. Couch the "quiet" yarn down the center of each bias strip between the fabric sections. Refer to Couching Basics (page 24).

Couch yarn down the center of each bias strip.

Other Options

- Add narrow raw-edge bias strips between the fabric sections. Center the strips with couched yarn.

- Couch your "quiet" yarn between fabric sections as desired.

Finishing the Fabric Sections

1. To conceal the outside edges of large embellished fabric sections, couch a double, twisted length of the "quiet" yarn.

Twist and couch 2 strands of yarn at the outside edges.

2. Add trim to cover the lapped zigzagged area on the back. The sample jacket used the female portion of snap tape trim, with a zipper foot and needle position feature to stitch it onto the jacket.

3. Trim the left shoulder with a row of twisted "quiet" yarn, bordered by 2 rows of your chosen trim (as shown, the male snap tape section).

Embellish the left shoulder with trim and yarn.

4. On the right shoulder, stitch your trim (male snap tape section) to cover and conceal the intersection of the front and back fabric embellishment.

Add trim where the front and back fabric sections meet.

5. Couch "quiet" yarn in the seamlines where the sleeves attach to the jacket body.

Finishing the Front and Hem Edges

tip

Construction rules of order to remember:

■ Finish horizontal hem edges before vertical center front edges.

■ Apply the neckline finish after the center front edges are completed.

1. Follow the directions for Wrapped Band Finishing (page 19). On the corners, miter the bias bands. Alternatively, you can attach the bias bands to the jacket in sections, leaving excess at both ends of each section and folding the extra length inward.

Apply these specifics to the hem finishing technique:

■ Use 1¾"-wide bias strips, cutting enough bias strips (see Bias Strip Magic, page 16) to do both sides of the front and the hemline, plus enough to fold inward at the beginning and ending points.

■ Sew ⅜" seams and then trim the seam allowance to ¼".

Since both trim and "loud" yarn will be added, just stitch in-the-ditch of the seam from the wrong side to hold the banding in place on the right side, using a straight stitch and monofilament thread in the needle.

On the right side, butt the trim to the stitching from the previous step. If you are using snap tape trim (as shown), use a zipper foot and take care to position the snaps so that you can stitch across the center fronts when finishing the neckline. Cut out the snap in the seam allowance to eliminate bulk at the neckline seam.

If you use snap tape, don't place metal where the collar stitching will go.

2. Couch your "loud" yarn along the outside edge of the trim or snap tape and your "quiet" yarn on the inside edge.

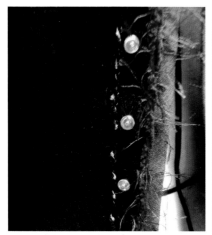

Couch yarn on both sides of the center front and hem bandings.

tip

If you are using Method 2 for fitting and construction, attach the jacket sleeves now, following the directions for Setting Sleeves (page 18).

Finishing the Sleeves

1. Cut the sleeves to the desired finished length.

2. Narrow the lower edge of the sleeve by stitching a 4½˝-long tuck as deep as works for the fit of your arm. (The sample jacket tuck was made by folding the sleeve lengthwise, across from the underarm seam, and stitching 1˝ from the fold.)

3. Press the tuck flat and stitch across the cut sleeve edge.

At the sleeve edge, flatten and stitch the tuck.

4. Stabilize the sleeve edge by applying Straight Fusible Stay Tape on the outside.

5. Follow the directions for Wrapped Band Finishing (page 19), embellishing with couched yarns the same as for the jacket body. Leave about 7˝ of loose yarn when beginning and ending your sleeve embellishment, tie these ends into a bow, and secure with hand stitching. Alternatively, thread the yarn ends on darning needles, pull to the inside, and bury them as explained in Couching Basics (page 24).

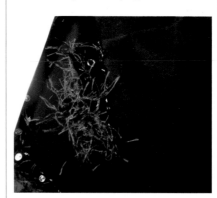

Finished sleeve edge, showing embellished finish and sleeve tuck

Making the Ribbing Collar

1. Measure the jacket neckline from one center front top edge around the back of the neck to the other front edge. Figure two-thirds of that measurement by multiplying by 0.66. That is the total length—tip to tip along the folded edge—to cut the bottom ribbing you previously removed from the sweatshirt. On the sample jacket, the jacket neckline was 39˝, so I multiplied by 0.66 to get 25¾˝ as the measurement to cut the ribbing.

2. Trim the seam edge off the ribbing, using a rotary cutter and ruler and leaving the ribbing as wide as possible. A width of 2˝–2¼˝ (double thickness) is typically available.

3. Cut one of the shorter ends into a curve, with the folded edge being the longer side.

4. Use a pin to mark the ribbing length determined in Step 1, measuring from the folded edge at the curved end. Fold the ribbing in half lengthwise, from the pin marker to the curved end, and use the cut curved edge as a pattern for cutting the other end.

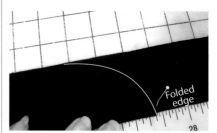

Use the curve you cut on the first end as a template to cut the other end exactly the same.

5. Mark the center of this length of ribbing with a pin. Mark the center back of the jacket neckline with a pin.

6. Open up the ribbing so that it is a single layer and place the *right* side of the ribbing against the *wrong* side of the jacket, matching the center of the ribbing to the center back of the jacket and aligning the raw edges. Pin together.

7. Match the opened end of the ribbing fold to the seamline (approximately ⅜″ on the jacket) at each center front. Pin in place.

Match the opened end of ribbing fold to the seamline at the jacket front. The photo shows the stitching line that will be made in Step 10.

8. Stretch the ribbing to match the neckline and secure with pins.

9. Repeat for the remaining half of the neckline, stretching the ribbing to match the jacket neckline.

Stretch the ribbing to fit the neckline and pin in place.

10. Stitch, utilizing the machine's needle-down function if available. Stitch with the ribbing on top so that you can see to manipulate the ribbing. Proper hand alignment at the machine is one hand in back, one in front. (Note the exact stitching in the photo under Step 7.)

11. The ribbing collar flips out and up so that the outside of the other layer of the ribbing can be stretched and pinned to the *outside* of the jacket. The neckline seam allowance will extend toward the fold of the ribbing.

12. Zigzag stitch the *raw cut edge* of the outside ribbing to the jacket through all the layers, using mono-filament thread in the needle.

Stretch, pin, and stitch the remaining outer layer edge in place, forcing the seam allowance toward the fold of the collar.

13. Carefully steam press; then finish by covering the raw edge with couching, using your "loud" yarn.

Adding a Closure

Stitch the button in place on the *left* jacket front. Test-fit, pin, and stitch a ponytail elastic to the inside of the *right* jacket front to create the closure mechanism for the button.

Stitch a ponytail elastic to the inside of the jacket to make a loop closure for the button.

Promised

Designed and made by Londa Rohlfing

SKILL LEVEL: *Medium*

FITTING: *Method 1*
or *Method 2*

Materials

- Basic Supplies (page 7)

- Sweatshirt (sized according to the fitting method you use), 80% cotton / 20% polyester

- 1 yard fabric for jacket outside neck facing, French facing, front bands, and cuffs

- 1 yard lightweight fabric for loop trim (both sides will show)

- 10 yards yarn for embellishment

- 2 large buttons (approximately 1″ diameter)

- 2 yards Knit Fusible Stay Tape

- 3 yards Straight Fusible Stay Tape

- 4.0/75 twin stretch sewing machine needle

- 3 jumbo snaps (additional snaps *optional*)

- Fabric Chenille Brush

Getting Started

Follow the steps for Preparing the Sweatshirt (page 8). You can make this jacket by either fitting technique. Method 1 (page 9) was used to make the sample jacket. If you use Method 2 (page 12), use pattern pieces 1, 2, 3, and 6.

These project instructions follow fitting Method 1; you will use tissue pattern piece 6 for the neckline. Fit the tissue first to decide if this exact neckline edge is good for you; alter the neckline if you wish. Cut the neckline of your sweatshirt.

Follow the directions for Stabilizing the Neckline (page 15).

Finishing the Hem

1. Fit to determine the finished jacket length you desire, turning under the excess and pinning at the center front, side seams, and center back. Measure to make sure that the length is exactly the same at the 2 side seams and at both center front edges.

2. To eliminate stretching, fuse Straight Fusible Stay Tape to the outside of both center front edges.

3. Following the directions for Twin-Needle Hemming (page 22), stabilize the hemline edge with Knit Fusible Stay Tape and stitch the hem.

Adding the Outside Neck Facing

1. Trace the neckline edge of your sweatshirt onto pattern tissue, marking the shoulder (yoke) seam on the tissue. At the back, mark the center back point.

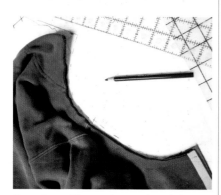

Trace the neckline on tissue and mark the yoke seamline.

2. Mark a width 4″ down from the neckline on the pattern tissue (1″ greater than the finished facing width). Cut the pattern apart at the marked shoulder line and add a ⅝″ seam allowance on each side of the cut.

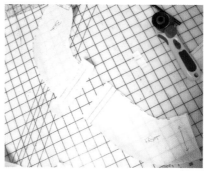

Cut 4″-wide facing templates, split, and add seam allowances.

3. Cut the facings from a double layer of facing fabric, right sides together. Position the back facing pattern with the center back line on a straight-grain fold of the fabric.

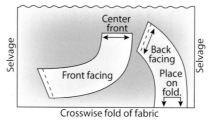

Cut front and back facings from doubled fabric.

4. Seam the front and back facings at the shoulders to make a single continuous neckline facing unit. Stitch around the unit ½″ from the larger arc of the facing. Press the edge to the wrong side of the fabric along the stitching line.

5. Pin the *wrong* side of the facing to the *right* side of the sweatshirt neckline, matching the shoulder (yoke) seams. Stitch together ⅜″ from the edge along the center front and neckline. (This seam will be covered with a neck band later.)

6. From the right side of the sweatshirt, secure the inner pressed edge to the sweatshirt with a *narrow* zigzag stitch (0.5 width and 3 length, on my machine), using monofilament thread in the needle.

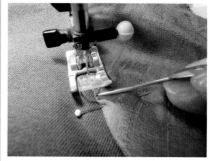

Use a Trolley Needle or stiletto to hold the pressed edge in place while stitching.

7. Embellish this neckline edge by couching yarn over the zigzag stitching—see Couching Basics (page 24).

Attaching the French Facing

1. Refer to Bias Strip Magic (page 16) to cut the neckline bias strip 3˝ wide and long enough plus 2˝, to cover the entire neckline edge, piecing if necessary.

2. Press the bias strip in half lengthwise, wrong sides together, creating a French facing.

3. Pin the French facing to the *right* side of the sweatshirt, having the raw strip edges aligned with the neckline edge and easing in the extra bias length at the curves. Stitch together with a scant ½˝ seam allowance.

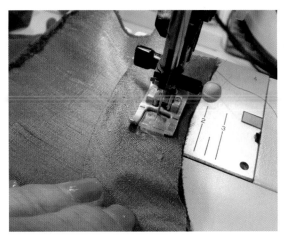

Stitch the banding in place, easing in the fullness around the back of the neck.

4. Clip the seam allowance of the concave curves perpendicular to the line of stitching. This is necessary so that the edge can expand when the banding is turned to the inside and this seam allowance edge becomes a longer convex curve.

> **tip**
>
> If your machine has needle positioning, use it to keep your seam allowance stitching even and align the fabric edge with the throat plate markings.

5. Press the bias band to the wrong side of the sweatshirt, coaxing the seamline to roll to the inside of the jacket. Pin to secure.

French facing seamline turns to the inside of the neckline.

6. From the inside of the jacket, stitch close to the folded edge of the bias. Make sure your bobbin thread matches the facing fabric on the outside of the jacket.

7. When finished, the outside neckline facing is approximately 2¾˝ wide on the outside of the jacket.

Finished neckline with French facing

Finishing the Center Front Edges

Follow the directions for Wrapped Band Finishing (page 19). The sample jacket's front bands were cut 5″ wide and 4″ longer than the jacket center front. Follow these directions for a nicely finished edge at the neckline:

1. *Using a ¾″ seam allowance, stitch the right side of the front bands to the wrong side of the sweatshirt fronts,* leaving at least ⅝″ excess band length at the bottom and 3″ at the neckline.

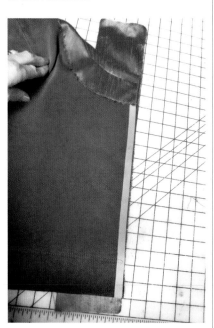

Sew the right side of the band to the wrong side of the sweatshirt.

2. Bring the band to the jacket front; turn under the long, raw edge of the band ½″; and press. Mark the finished neckline edge on the front bands with chalk; then open the band away from the jacket front and stitch along the chalked line, stitching only through the single layer of front band fabric. Do this on each side of the jacket front.

Mark the neckline edge on both front bands.

3. Trim the band to ½″ above the stitching and fold the remaining top edge under, turning the inside corner in at an angle. Slipstitch the folds together by hand along the neckline and the depth of the neckline facing.

Turn under the trimmed front band excess and slipstitch. Note the angled fold of the corner.

4. Refer to Couching Basics (page 24) to couch yarn along the inner edges of the center front bands, starting at the couched edge of the neckline.

Couch yarn along the front bands as shown.

Making the Loop Trim

1. Experiment to decide on the spacing and length you want for your bias loop trim. (The sample jacket has 3¼″ of trim attached every 1¼″.) Place pins along the neckline facing and front bands to mark the spacing you've decided on; count the number of pins.

2. Figure out how much bias loop trim is needed by multiplying the length of fabric in each loop (3¼″ on the sample jacket) by the number of pins in Step 1. To this measurement, add at least 46″ more for the front tie trim, plus some extra, just in case.

3. Refer to Bias Strip Magic (page 16) to cut bias trim 1¾˝ wide to the length you calculated in Step 2. Piece strips as needed, as instructed in Bias Strip Magic, Steps 6–8. Stitch on tissue paper to prevent stretching, keeping the beginnings and endings of your stitching lines neat. You'll need to create plenty of length, but it needn't be in a single continuous strip as the loop trim will break at the center front neckline.

4. On your long bias trim, measure and mark loop spacing (3¼˝ on the sample jacket) in both directions from any piecing seams to ensure that loop piecing seams are at points that will be stitched to the jacket rather than will be exposed in the loops themselves.

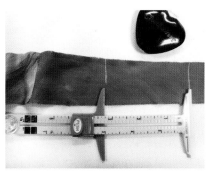

Mark your loop spacing in each direction from seams.

5. Use the Fabric Chenille Brush to slightly rough up each side of the bias loop trim.

Gently brush each edge of the bias trim.

6. Match the first marking on the bias loop trim to the first pin markings on the jacket. Position the bias loop trim so that approximately ½˝ of facing shows on each side of the trim.

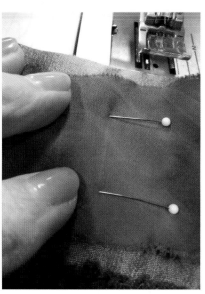

Pin so approximately ½˝ of the base fabric shows on each side.

7. Continue to match the markings on the bias loop trim to the pin markings on the jacket, breaking the trim at the center front neckline; pin in place. At the bottom edge, loop under the trim flush with the hemline at the center front. At the center back, make an additional loop.

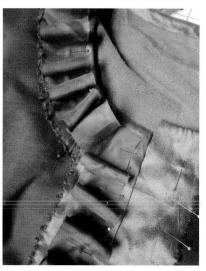

Match the pins on the jacket to the chalk markings on the trim.

Make an extra loop of bias trim at the center back.

8. Secure the bias loop trim to the jacket, using monofilament thread in the needle and stitching across *only the center 1˝* of the looped trim at each marking, securing your stitches.

Sew across only the center of each loop attachment point.

9. Gently steam press the loops so that they lie softly flat by hovering a steam iron over them and gently pressing them with the palm of your hand. Press the neckline loops outward in each direction from the center back loop and toward the center in front. Press the jacket front loops downward.

The trim at left is stitched but not pressed; the loops at right have been softly steam pressed.

10. To make bias hanging tails to go under the buttons at center front, cut 2 pieces of the bias loop trim approximately 18˝ long. Fold in half crosswise and turn in the folded corners at an angle.

Fold 18˝ lengths of bias loop trim in half and fold as shown.

11. Tack the folds by machine to the upper center front neckline edges so that buttons will cover the stitching. Stitch the buttons in place by hand, making long shanks and tying the bias fabric around them.

Sew on the buttons and tie the thread tails around the button shanks.

Stitching the Front Closure

Establish the placement for hanging invisible snaps (page 21) as the center front closure. Position a top snap ½˝ from the neckline, another snap at bust level, and additional snaps as desired. These won't be visible, so functionality is more important here than equal spacing. Mark the placement with a chalk line across both fronts on the inside of the jacket and attach the snaps.

> *tip* ··
>
> If you are using Method 2 for fitting and constructing the jacket, attach the sleeves now, following the directions for Setting Sleeves (page 18).

Finishing the Sleeves

Determine an attractive finished sleeve length and cut both sleeves to that length. Follow the directions for Wrapped Band Finishing (page 19) to attach bias sleeve bands. (The bands on the sample jacket were cut 5˝ wide and stitched to the sleeves with a ⅝˝ seam allowance.)

Captured

Designed and made by Londa Rohlfing

Materials

- Basic Supplies (page 7)

- Sweatshirt (size 2X), 80% cotton / 20% polyester

- 1¾ yards feature fabric (44˝ wide) for bands and collar (*or* 1½ yards fabric, 60˝ wide)

- ⅝ yard lightweight fabric (such as silk organza) for casing and under collar*

- 8–10 yards yarn for embellishment

- ¼ yard woven fusible interfacing

- 4 yards Straight Fusible Stay Tape

- 3 large buttons (approximately 1¼˝ diameter)

- 1 small safety pin

- 8 medium-sized safety pins

- 70 denim/sharp or microtex needle and 75 stretch needle

* If your feature fabric is lightweight enough, you can simply add to that amount for the casing strip and under collar.

Getting Started

Use pattern pieces 1–5 for this project. Fit and construct this jacket according to Method 2 (page 12), using the front neckline designated as *Captured* on pattern piece 1 for this design.

1. Follow the steps for Preparing the Sweatshirt (page 8).

2. Stay the shoulder seams by fusing Straight Fusible Stay Tape along the seamlines on the jacket fronts. Stitch the back to the fronts at the shoulder seams, placing the back toward the feed dogs to ease in the back shoulder fullness.

Stitch the shoulder seams, easing in the back fullness.

3. Follow the steps for Stabilizing the Neckline (page 15).

4. Fuse Straight Fusible Stay Tape to the right side of the fabric along both center front edges.

5. Stitch the side seams. Finish the seam allowances by serging or using a wide and long zigzag stitch. Press toward the back.

Finishing the Hem

1. To create the hem band, cut a straight-grain strip of the feature fabric 2½″ wide and as long as the bottom hem. Cut interfacing the same length and 2″ wide. Center and fuse the interfacing on the *wrong* side of the fabric strip.

Fuse the interfacing to the wrong side of the hem band.

2. Press the hem band in half lengthwise, wrong sides together.

3. Fit the jacket and mark the desired length, taking into account the 1″ that the hem band will add to the jacket length. Allowing for a ⅜″ seam, cut off the excess at the bottom edge of the jacket. Apply Straight Fusible Stay Tape to the *wrong* side of this edge of the jacket.

4. Lay the hem band on the *right* side of the jacket at the hemline, matching the cut edges. Pin and stitch with a ⅜″ seam.

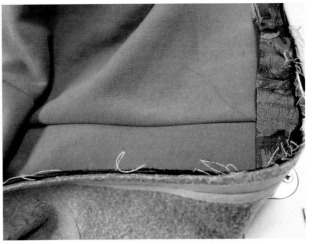

Stitch the hem band to the bottom edge of the jacket.

5. Finish the raw edge of the hem band by serging, by using a 3-step zigzag stitch, or by binding with a lightweight fabric.

6. Press the hem band down, away from the jacket.

7. Refer to Couching Basics (page 24) to couch yarn around the jacket bottom in the well of the seam.

Finishing the Front Edges

1. Follow the directions for Wrapped Band Finishing (page 19), using the following measurements:

■ For the front bands, cut 2 strips of the feature fabric (on either straight or bias grain) 3½″ wide and 3″ longer than the center front jacket edges.

■ Stitch the bands to the jacket fronts with a ¾″ seam, leaving at least ½″ excess band length at the bottom and plenty of extra length at the top.

2. Couch yarn to embellish the inner edge of the front bands.

3. Cut off the excess front banding at the neckline along the angle of the jacket's V neckline, leaving a raw edge to be finished later.

Finishing the Sleeves

tip ....

The directions for finishing the sleeves are placed early in the construction process for this jacket to serve as practice in gathering before you attack the collar edges. For complete directions for my gathering technique, see Making Gathers (page 17).

1. Pin the sleeve to the jacket to determine an attractive finished length. The given measurements for the puffed sleeve band add 2″ in length, but these can be adjusted by changing the band width in the following step.

2. From the feature fabric, cut 2 *bias* pieces, 4″ wide by 1½ times the length of the lower sleeve edge. These will be the upper puffed sections.

3. For the facing sections, from either the lightweight fabric or the feature fabric, cut 2 *straight-grain* pieces 3″ wide by the length of the lower edge of the sleeve *plus 1″*.

4. Fuse Straight Fusible Stay Tape along the lower edge of the sweatshirt sleeve on the *wrong* side.

5. As described in Making Gathers (page 17), sew 2 rows of gathering stitches along one long edge of the upper puffed sections and then join to the sleeve hem edge, right sides together. The ends of the puffed sections will be even with the underarm edge of the sleeves. Your seam allowance is ⅝″.

Gather and attach one edge of the puffed section to the sleeve.

6. Gather and attach the free edge of the puffed section to a long edge of a facing section, right sides together.

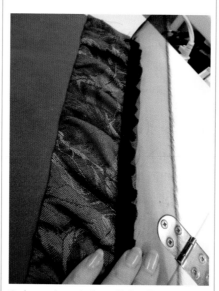

Gather and attach the puffed cuff section.

7. Open up the puffed and facing sections and stitch the underarm sleeve seam, using a ⅝″ seam allowance and continuing the stitching through the puffed section and the facing. Take care to exactly match the horizontal seams of the puffed section with the facing.

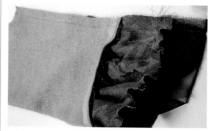

Stitch at the underarm and through the puffed section and facing.

8. Clip into the seam allowance at the bottom edge of the sleeve fabric. Trim and serge or zigzag the sleeve seam allowance above your clip. Press the seam toward the front of the sleeve. Below the clip, press open the seam allowance in the puffed section and facing.

Clip so that you can press open the seam allowance at the bottom.

9. Utilizing the free arm of your sewing machine, turn under the free facing edge ¼″ and align folded edge where the puffed section joins the sleeve; zigzag stitch to secure.

Zigzag stitch the facing on the inside of the sleeve.

10. On the outside, couch yarn to cover the last stitching line and embellish the sleeve edge.

Couch yarn to cover the facing seam.

11. Insert the sleeves into the jacket body according to the instructions for Setting Sleeves (page 18).

Making the Collar

1. Cut the under collar piece from your lightweight fabric, placing the pattern's center back edge on the fold of doubled fabric.

Cut the upper collar from your feature fabric, positioning the center back on a crosswise fold if you are using 44″ fabric. Only with 60″ fabric can you place the upper collar on a lengthwise fold of fabric.

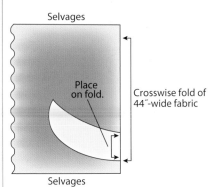

Selvages

Place on fold.

Crosswise fold of 44″-wide fabric

Selvages

For 44″ fabric, cut the upper collar on a *crosswise* fold.

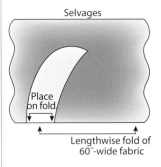

Selvages

Place on fold.

Lengthwise fold of 60″-wide fabric

For 60″ fabric, cut the upper collar on a *lengthwise* fold.

2. Securely mark both the upper and under collar pieces at these points, using medium-sized safety pins:

- Shoulder seam, at both the neckline and the outer edges
- Center back, at both the neckline and the outer edges

3. On the upper collar, *also* mark the following:

- On the right side of the fabric, the buttonhole placement
- On the wrong side of the fabric, the casing placement line

4. Center and fuse 2 squares 1½″ × 1½″ of fusible interfacing to the *wrong* side of the upper collar at the buttonhole markings.

5. With a sharp needle in the sewing machine, make a ½″ buttonhole at each center front buttonhole marking on the upper collar. Refer to the pattern piece for the exact placement. Carefully slash the buttonholes open.

6. To create the casing strip, refer to Bias Strip Magic (page 16) to cut a 70″ bias length of the lightweight fabric 1″ wide so that it will curve with the collar shape. (I used silk organza for this.) Piece as necessary by overlapping and stitching the 1″ strips of casing fabric until you have a strip long enough to span the casing line of the upper collar.

7. Center the casing strip over the casing placement line marked on the *wrong side* of the upper collar. The strip should cover the buttonhole at each front collar point. Pin in place, being careful *not* to stretch it as you work.

8. Stitch about ⅛″ from one side, using a 2.0 stitch length. Stitch the other side ½″ from the first stitching line to create the casing tunnel.

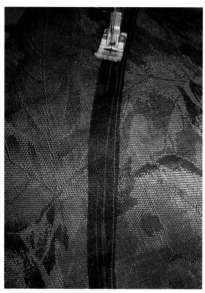

Stitch the casing strip to the wrong side of the upper collar.

tip

To create an evenly stitched casing, it is actually easiest to keep your eye on the right side of the presser foot when you sew the second stitching line. Watch to make sure the presser foot stays the same distance from the first stitching line. Equidistant spacing is more important than where the stitching lands on the casing strip—just so long as it is even and secure. This stitching *will show* on the right side of the collar.

Creating the Teeny Cord

1. Cut a bias strip of the feature fabric 1″ wide and approximately 85″ long. It will take at least 2 strips of fabric to yield the length you need. Keep it in 2 pieces and make 2 separate cords, as it is easier to turn a shorter length. They will be stitched together to create a single long piece.

tip

The strip for the cord doesn't have to be cut on a true 45° bias—close to bias will work fine.

2. Adjust your stitch length to a small stitch (1.5 on my machine). Fold the strip lengthwise, right sides together, and stitch a scant ¼″ from the raw edge, stretching the strip as you stitch. At the start, angle your stitching in from the raw edges to make a funnel-shaped opening at the end.

Start stitching with a ⅛″ seam allowance and "funnel" the seam allowance to a scant ¼″ to facilitate turning the cord.

tip

Stretch the strip with one hand behind the needle and one hand in front as you sew. This is necessary so that when the cord gets pulled, the stitching won't break.

3. Thread a large, strong needle with a double strand of strong polyester thread (or even buttonhole thread). Knot the end and stitch through the fold of the strip's wide end—several times so that it is very secure.

4. Guide the *eye* end of the needle down through the tube of fabric until it comes out the other end as a cord. The fabric at the beginning will start to turn. Pull on the thread until the fabric end is pulled through; then switch and pull on the turned fabric end instead of the thread until the cord is completely turned right side out.

Pull the thread until you see turned fabric; then pull the fabric to finish turning the cord.

5. Machine stitch repeatedly to securely join the 2 cord sections into 1 long cord. This stitching won't be seen—it will be hidden inside the collar casing.

6. With the small-sized safety pin attached to one end, guide this cord through the casing, entering and exiting through the buttonholes at the collar front corners.

Guide the cord into the buttonhole and through the casing.

Joining the Collars

1. Sew gathering stitches along the neckline edge and the outer edge of the upper collar, breaking your stitching at the center back fold and shoulder seams (marked with safety pins) to make 4 sections of gathering stitches along the neckline and 4 sections along the outer edge. Refer to Making Gathers (page 17). Your seam allowance is ⅜″.

2. With right sides together, pin the upper collar to the under collar *along the outer edge only,* lining up the center backs and shoulder line markings. Pull the threads to gather the upper collar to fit the under collar. Pin, distributing the fullness. Stitch between the gathering rows and carefully trim the seam to ⅜″.

Gather the upper collar to fit the under collar and stitch.

3. Open the seam from the right side of the upper collar and force the trimmed seam allowance toward the under collar. Secure by stitching through the right side of the under collar and the seam allowances close to the seam. This is called *understitching.*

Sheer layer of silk organza as under collar

Understitch to secure the seam allowance to the under collar.

4. With wrong sides together, pin the upper collar to the under collar at the neckline edge, matching the center back and shoulder line markings. Gather the upper collar to fit the under collar and pin. Stitch.

Gather and stitch the upper collar to the under collar at the neckline edge.

Attaching the Collar

1. Pin the collar to the jacket neckline, with the *right* side of the under collar to the *right* side of the jacket, matching the center back, shoulder markings, and center front edges. Machine baste along the ⅜″ seamline.

2. From your feature fabric, cut a 2″-wide bias strip that is 2″ longer than the neckline edge.

3. Leaving 1″ excess bias strip on each side at the center front, pin the *right* side of the bias strip to the *right* side of the upper collar and stitch a ⅜″ seam though all the layers. Trim the seam allowance and clip in at the curves.

Stitch the bias strip to the upper collar at the neckline.

4. Press the bias strip outward, away from the collar. Understitch by stitching the seam allowance to the bias strip close to the seam on the right side of the fabric.

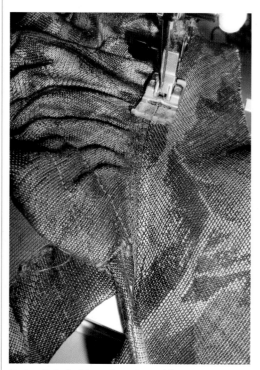

Understitch the bias strip at the neckline.

5. Flip the bias strip down into place on the inside of the jacket. Turn under the long raw edge and the ends at the center fronts. Keeping the collar free, stitch through all the layers to secure the edge to the jacket neckline. Slipstitch the ends in place at the center front.

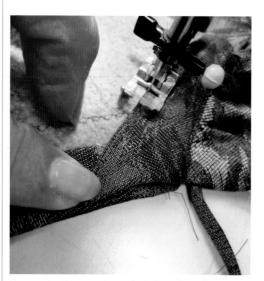

Turn under the raw edge and stitch to the jacket at the neckline.

Finishing the Jacket

1. Sew a large button right on top of the upper collar at the left front, where the cord exits, keeping the cord free so you can adjust the gathers of the collar.

Stitch a button on the left front collar.

2. Pull the cord through the right side of the collar, distributing fullness nicely. Leave at least 9″ of the cord emerging from the buttonhole on the left jacket side. Knot the end of the cord and allow it to freely dangle.

3. Fit the jacket to check the distribution of the collar fullness. Mark the bust level for the placement of the second button; then mark the third button location an equal distance below that. Stitch the buttons on the jacket.

4. Stitch to anchor the cord at the right front side of the collar near the buttonhole.

5. Experiment with twirling the cord around the buttons to create loop closures and embellishment down the right jacket band. Pin the loops in place. Try on the jacket again to make sure the loops will hold the buttons on the left side of the jacket.

Twirl, knot, and twist the cording to create button loops and embellishment.

6. With monofilament thread both on top and in the bobbin, anchor-stitch the cord as designed to the right side of the jacket. Allow the last segment of the cord to dangle freely with a knot in the end.

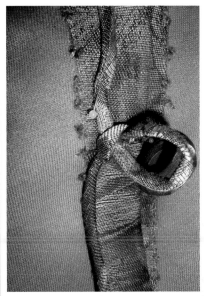

Invisibly stitch the cord to the jacket.

7. Put on the jacket and have a helper check to make sure the fullness of the collar lies correctly in back, with no under collar showing. Pin the collar to the sweatshirt as desired. From the inside, anchor the collar by hand stitching *only* through the sweatshirt and under collar.

Tack the fullness of the collar in place around the back of the jacket.

Innovative

Designed and made by Londa Rohlfing

Materials

- Basic Supplies (page 7)

- Sweatshirt (sized according to the fitting method you use), 80% cotton / 20% polyester

- 1 yard print fabric for inside front jacket bands and pieced front bands (Fabric A)

- 1 yard coordinating fabric for hem, collar/sleeve edging, and facings (Fabric B)

- ½ yard *each* of 5 additional coordinating fabrics for pieced front bands

- ¾ yard lightweight fabric (silk organza) for base of pieced sections

- 10–15 yards yarn for embellishing

- 4 yards Straight Fusible Stay Tape

- ⅜ yard interfacing, woven stitch-in, or woven fusible

- 2 safety pins

- 5 buttons, at least 1″ diameter

> **DESIGN NOTE**
>
> *If you are using a stripe as your subordinate accent Fabric B, a yarn-dyed reversible fabric will make it possible to form a chevron pattern for the lower bandings. Additional fabric will be needed to match the pattern.*

Getting Started

Fit the jacket according to your preferred fitting technique (page 8). Method 2 (page 12) was used for the jacket in the photographs. If using Method 2, use pattern pieces 1, 2, 3, and 6. If using Method 1 (page 9), use pattern piece 6 for the *Innovative* neckline.

Follow the steps for Preparing the Sweatshirt (page 8). Keep the bottom ribbing for use on a future jacket, though you won't need it for this one. Follow the instructions for Stabilizing the Neckline (page 15).

> **DESIGN NOTE**
>
> **Important!** *Regardless of which fitting technique you use, do not cut the sweatshirt at the center front! Follow the directions below to locate an attractive offset front closure location based on your body. When cutting, be sure to follow the proper front neckline on pattern piece 6 for this design.*

Designing and Stitching the Front Opening

1. If you are using Method 1 as your fitting technique, leave the center front *uncut*. If you are using Method 2, cut the front according to the pattern at the neckline, shoulder, armhole, and sides, but *leave as much width as the sweatshirt fabric allows at the center front.* Fitting Method 2 was used for the sample jacket with the following directions.

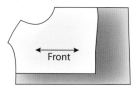

Cut the jacket pieces but leave them as wide as possible at the center front.

2. Hold the front section of the jacket up to the body to decide where you want the off-center right front edge. *Caution:* Be sure to locate this edge at least 1½″ *toward the center* from the left bust point so that you don't end up with a button exactly at the bust apex. On the jacket in the photos, this edge is approximately 5″ to the left of center. Mark this with a straight line the length of the jacket from neckline to bottom edge.

3. Clip in just ¼″ at the neckline to mark the actual center front. Cut the front section into 2 pieces at the offset line established in Step 2.

4. Apply Straight Fusible Stay Tape to the *right* side of both front edges.

Fuse stay tape to the front edges on the outside.

5. To make the front extension section, cut 3 pieces 5″ wide and 5″ longer than the center front cut edges from Fabric A.

Cut 3 finishing pieces for the center front edges.

DESIGN NOTE

Fabric A on the sample jacket had a horizontal stripe effect. To achieve the impression of a vertical stripe, these pieces were cut on the cross grain. If this isn't a factor, cut your strips on the lengthwise grain.

6. Cut interfacing and fuse to the wrong side of one of the 5″-wide strips. This will become the outer layer of the underlap on the jacket left front.

7. Position the interfaced piece to an uninterfaced piece, right sides together, and stitch one long edge with a ½″ seam allowance. Press flat to seal the seam, press the seam open, and press the pieces wrong sides together.

"Seal" the seam by pressing it flat as stitched.

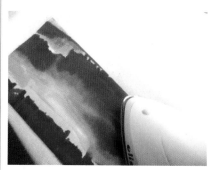

Press the pieces closed, with the seam lying exactly on the edge.

tip

The steps in these photographs are the key to getting any seam on an edge to *really* lie nicely.

8. Stitch the *right* side of the uninterfaced front extension piece of this unit to the *wrong* side of the left front edge using a ½″ seam allowance, stopping about 4″ from the bottom edge. (This will allow you to complete the hem before you finish the front.)

Stitch the uninterfaced edge of the unit to the left front, stopping 4″ from the bottom.

9. Wrap the extension section around the seam allowance and press under the innermost edge ¼″. Pin in place, stopping 4″ from the bottom edge.

Bring the interfaced section of the band to the front of the jacket piece.

Stitching the Jacket Body

1. Stitch the side seams with a ⅝″ seam allowance, serging or finishing the raw edges with a 3-step zigzag stitch (6 wide, 5 long are the approximate settings on my machine). Press toward the back.

2. Mark the bust points with safety pins. This will be helpful when you design the embellishment.

3. Stitch the underarm sleeve seams and finish the same as the side seams. Press toward the front.

4. Insert the sleeves into the jacket, following the directions for Setting Sleeves (page 18).

5. Fit the jacket to determine an attractive body length, allowing for a 1″ band to be added at the bottom edge. Mark the jacket hem ½″ longer at the center back. Cut evenly to this length.

Creating Stitch-and-Flip Bands

1. Cut a number of 6″-long pieces in various widths from all 7 fabrics. The pieces on the sample jacket vary from ⅞″ to 2″ wide.

Cut 6″ strips in different widths.

2. You'll sew the fabric pieces from Step 1 onto foundation pieces of lightweight fabric. From the lightweight fabric cut the following pieces:

- 6″ × sleeve edge length, for cuffs (Cut 2.)

- 6″ × right jacket front length, for right front band

- 6″ × at least 33″, for upper collar

3. At the left end of one of the lightweight base pieces, stitch a fabric piece right side *up,* stitching a scant ¼″ in and along both of the 6″ sides.

4. Pin the next selected fabric right side *down* on top of first piece, aligning the 6″ edges on the right. Stitch a ¼″ seam. Flip this piece in place, right side up, and press the seam.

5. Repeat Steps 3 and 4, alternating strip widths and colors, until each lightweight base fabric is covered.

Alternate 6″ strips and stitch to the base fabric, pressing after you flip each piece in place.

6. Trim both long edges of each completed piece to use for the front band, the collar, and 2 cuffs to measure exactly 5½″ wide.

Trim each band to 5½″ wide.

Attaching the Right Front Band

1. Stitch the *right* side of the pieced front band to the *wrong* side of the jacket right front, following the steps for Wrapped Band Finishing (page 19), with the following specifics:

- Stitch a ½″ seam, stopping 4″ from the bottom edge.

- Trim the seam allowance to ¼″ and turn the band to the outside of the jacket, wrapping the pieced section around the seam allowance.

Trim the seam to ¼″ and wrap the front band to the outside.

Press the wrapped edge from inside the jacket, allowing ¼″ of the pieced band to show on the inside of the jacket.

2. Try on the jacket to decide how wide to design the right front band. The band on the sample jacket is 3¾″ wide. Measure from the center wrapped edge to mark the width you have designed.

3. Cut the front band ½″ wider than the marked width. Press under the extra ½″ and pin in place on the outside of the jacket, stopping 4″ from the bottom edge.

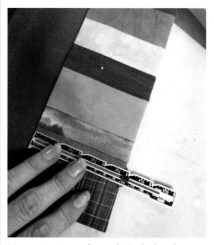

Measure, press under, and pin the band in place.

4. From the inside, cut off the excess fabric at the top of the front band, following the jacket neckline, leaving a raw edge.

5. Staystitch the right front neckline edge through the sweatshirt and the front band layers.

Finishing the Hem

1. Stabilize the bottom edge by applying Straight Fusible Stay Tape on the *wrong* side of the jacket, close to the edge.

2. From Fabric B, cut a hem extension bias 3¼″ wide and the length of only the sweatshirt hemline *plus* 1″. Piece if necessary, placing any seams to correspond with the side or center back seams of the jacket.

3. Cut fusible interfacing 3″ wide and the same length as the hem extension. Center the interfacing, sticky side down, on the *wrong* side of the hem extension; fuse.

4. Press the hem extension in half lengthwise, wrong sides together.

5. Lay the folded hem extension along the right side of the jacket fabric, matching raw edges. Stitch with a ⅜″ seam. Trim the sweatshirt edge of the seam allowance to reduce bulk. Serge or 3-step zigzag to finish the raw edge.

6. Press the hem extension away from the jacket body with the seam allowance toward the jacket body. Refer to Couching Basics (page 24) to couch yarn along the seamline on the outside to hold the hem extension down in place.

Finishing the Front Edges

1. When the bottom edge of the jacket is finished, stitch the last 4″ of the jacket left front extension piece, sewing across the hem extension.

2. Fold in ½″ on the inner edge of the left front extension. Zigzag stitch in place, using monofilament thread in the needle. Wrap the edge and finish according to the directions for Wrapped Band Finishing (page 19). Couch yarn to cover the stitching.

3. Finish stitching the last 4″ of the right front stitch-and-flip piece, stitching across the hem extension.

4. Wrap the edge and finish according to the directions for Wrapped Band Finishing (page 19). Couch yarn along the inside edge of the right front band.

Wrapped and couched front bands and hemline

Attaching the Cuffs

1. Apply Straight Fusible Stay Tape to the outside of each sleeve edge.

2. Determine the finished sleeve length so that the sleeves are either longer or shorter than the finished jacket hemline when the arms are held at the sides.

3. Decide on an attractive finished width for the pieced cuffs and cut the pieced cuff sections 1″ wider than this measurement. (The finished cuffs on the sample jacket are 3½″ wide, so the pieces were cut 4½″ wide.)

4. From Fabric B, cut 2 bias cuff facings 1″ wider than the cuff pieces, with the length being the circumference of the sleeve. (On the sample jacket, they were cut 5½″ wide.) Refer to the Design Note about directional prints for bands (page 19).

5. Align the pieced cuffs with the cuff facings with right sides together along one long edge and stitch together using a ½˝ seam allowance. Trim the seam allowance arrow-straight and even. Press the seam allowance toward the cuff facing. Wrap the facing around the seam allowance to bring the raw edges of the cuff facing and the pieced cuff together evenly.

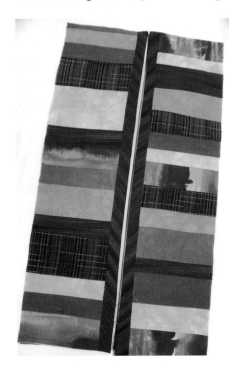

6. Open up the facings and with right sides together stitch each cuff into a tube that is equal to the length of the finished sleeve edge circumference. Press the seam open.

7. Stitch the *right* side of the facing to the *wrong* side of the sleeve lower edge with a ½˝ seam allowance. Press the seam down toward the cuff.

Stitch the right side of the cuff facing to the wrong side of the sleeve.

8. Flip the pieced cuff into place on the outside of the sleeve. Turn under the remaining top cuff edge and zigzag in place, using monofilament thread in the needle.

9. Couch yarn to cover and embellish the top cuff edge. Bury the yarn ends using a darning needle, as shown in Couching Basics (page 24).

Designing the Neckline

This neckline can be as high or as low as you desire. The photos and captions below show how the neckline on the sample jacket was made lower. Play designer—it's fun!

1. Pin the right side of the pieced upper collar to the wrong side of the jacket, placing the pins parallel to the neckline edge.

Pin the collar in place.

2. Decide how much you want to lower the neckline at the jacket (real) center front. Pin to mark.

The sample jacket neckline was lowered 2″ at the center front.

3. Decide if also lowering the neckline at the center back would be beneficial to eliminate the double locker patch stitching. The sample jacket neckline was lowered 1″ at the center back.

Check to see if the collar can cover the locker patch on the jacket back.

4. Unpin and remove the upper collar. Fold the jacket, wrong sides together, along the original center front and center back lines.

5. Mark a new neckline cutting line, allowing for a ⅝″ seam allowance. Cut off any excess in a smooth curve.

6. Staystitch the neckline edge of the sweatshirt *except* for the left front extension.

Finishing the Left Front Neckline

1. Clip the sweatshirt seam allowance to the stay stitching where the left front extension joins the jacket.

2. Turn the inside of the facing side of the left front extension to the *outside*. With right sides together, stitch along the top neckline edge ⅝″ from the raw edge. Trim the seam allowance to ¼″, cutting at an angle across the corner.

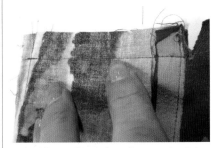

Clip to the stitching where the extension joins the jacket.

3. Turn the extension facing to the inside. Press to finish the left front extension at the neckline, where no collar will be attached.

Finished look of left neckline and front extension

Making the Collar

1. Measure your new neckline edge and add 3″ to this length. Make sure you have a pieced upper collar at least that long.

2. From Fabric B, cut an under collar facing 1″ wider than the upper collar and the length of the pieced upper collar from Step 1. The sample upper collar is 5½″ wide, so the under collar was cut 6½″ wide.

3. With right sides together, pin the upper collar to the under collar along one long edge. Stitch a ½″ seam. Trim your seam to be exact, as you did for the cuffs. Press the seam allowance toward the under collar and wrap the under collar around the seam allowance, similar to the cuffs.

4. Pin the right side of the under collar to the right side of the upper collar at both short front ends. Allow the 1″ of excess under collar width to extend beyond the width of the pieced collar section.

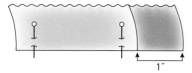

A short end of the pieced upper collar is pinned to a short end of the under collar with the extra width of the under collar beyond the pin on the right.

5. Allow the short ends of the collar to extend ½″ beyond the front edges of the jacket, and pin the collar to the jacket at the neck, with the right side of the upper collar attached to the wrong side of the jacket. Ease any extra collar length into the back neckline as you pin. Stitch a ½″ seam and press the seam allowance toward the collar.

6. To finish the front ends, push the excess under collar width toward the cut long lower edge; pin.

Fold the extra under collar width toward the long stitched edge.

7. With the wrong side of the upper collar facing up at the sewing machine—to enable equidistant stitching from the last stitch-and-flip piecing line—stitch each end flush with the finished edges of the jacket fronts.

8. Turn and press the collar, wrapping the lower seam allowance with the excess collar width.

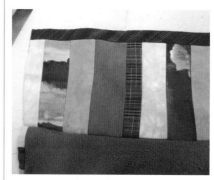

Finished collar end, shown from inside the right front edge

9. Turn under the neckline edge of the under collar, pin, and slipstitch to the jacket neckline edge on the outside of the jacket, underneath the collar.

10. Couch yarn over the seam of the lower collar banding, burying the ends as explained in Couching Basics (page 24).

Creating Closures

1. From Fabric B, cut a strip 1½″ wide to make into loop closures for the buttons. For the sample jacket, 4″ per button was allowed (20″ for all 5 buttons called for in the materials list). Depending on your button size, you may need more or less. This strip may be cut on the straight grain or the bias. (I cut mine on the straight grain because of the lines of the fabric.)

2. With right sides together, stitch the long edges together, using only a ⅛″ seam allowance for the first 1″ and then angling to a ¼″ seam allowance for the remaining strip length.

Stitch the strip with a wider opening at one end to facilitate turning the cord.

3. Turn this tube right side out by inserting a loop turner at the narrow end and hooking into a good bite of fabric fold at the funnel-shaped end.

4. Fit the jacket to determine the best button placement, locating the top button right at the collar intersection and another button at the bust level. Mark the desired button placement.

Mark the desired button placement on the jacket front.

5. Sew the buttons onto the left front at your placement markings.

Sew on the buttons and mark the loop positions.

6. Experiment to determine how long a loop is needed for each button. (For the sample jacket's 1″-diameter buttons, 3″ loops were needed.) Cut loops this length and pin in place on the wrong side of the right front edge.

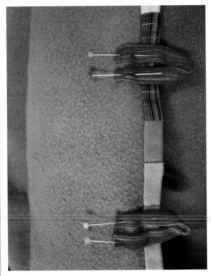

Pin loops to the wrong side of the right front.

7. On the wrong side, attach the button loops by stitching in-the-ditch of the seam where the embellished right front joins the sweatshirt.

Stitch in-the-ditch to attach the button loops.

8. After pressing the loops so they extend to the right side, on the outside couch yarn to conceal the loop stitching and to add embellishment, leaving 7″ yarn ends at the neck and hem edges. Bury the yarn ends as described in Couching Basics (page 24).

Cover and embellish the stitching line with yarn.

9. On the inside of the jacket, turn under the ends of the loops and stitch by hand to secure.

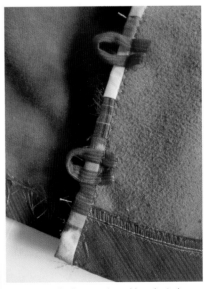

Turn under the loop ends and hand stitch to the jacket.

InVested

Designed and made by Londa Rohlfing

72

SKILL LEVEL: *Challenging*

FITTING: *Method 2*

Materials

- Basic Supplies (page 7)

- Sweatshirt (size 2XL), 80% cotton / 20% polyester

- ½ yard *each* of 2 coordinating fabrics for embellishment

- Jeans (a large size yields the most fabric; men's 40/30 long was used for the sample jacket)

- Heavy-duty zipper, the desired length of the center front (24″ on the sample jacket)

- 4 yards Straight Fusible Stay Tape

- Denim sewing machine needle, size 100

- 10–15 yards yarn for embellishment

Getting Started

Fit this jacket according to Method 2 (page 12), using pattern pieces 1 and 2 and following the front neckline on the pattern tissue for this design.

Remove the sleeves from the sweatshirt (reserve the fabric for other projects) and then follow the steps for Preparing the Sweatshirt (page 8). Be sure to retain the bottom ribbing to use for the jacket neckline and the cuff ribbings to use for the armhole finishing.

Designing the Yokes

It's fun and easy to sketch your own yoke embellishment sections. When you are happy with your design, just "eyeball" the lines on your sweatshirt pieces and mark them with chalk. Lay the embellishment fabric on these areas, cutting it at least ½″ larger on all sides to allow for clean finished edges.

In the photos, note how I laid down the fabric and then lifted it to insert pins along the chalked design lines to define them on the right side of the fabric. Then I simply cut the sections ½″ away from the pins. The grain of the embellishment fabric doesn't matter.

1. Pin your uppermost fabric on the right upper front yoke, with its bottom edge extending ½″ below the chalked design line.

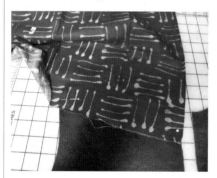

2. Turn over to cut the fabric along the neckline, shoulder, and armhole edges.

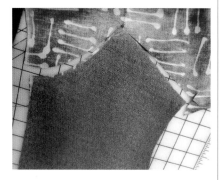

3. Darken your chalk lines for the 2 lower fabric sections, which intersect at the center front.

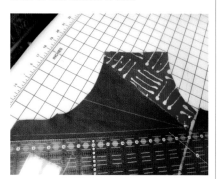

4. Cut the center piece. Turn under the upper edge and pin in place. Mark the bottom design line with pins.

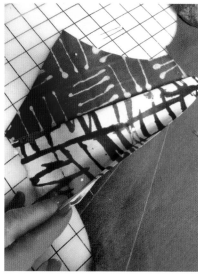

5. Turn under the top edge of the bottom fabric and pin in place. Chalk the lower edge line.

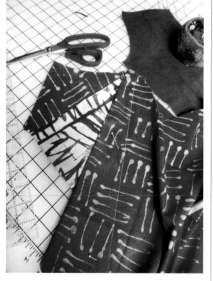

6. Cut the last piece ½˝ larger, turn under, and pin in place.

7. Designed upper yoke—simple!

8. Flip the entire piece over and trim the fabric along the sweatshirt edges at the neckline, center front, and armhole.

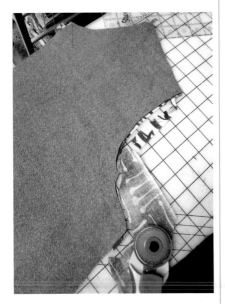

DESIGN NOTE

With everything pinned in place so far, I knew I wanted to integrate some denim from the jeans. Before I could do that, I needed to cut the lower jeans unit. Jumping around as you design is normal operating procedure. Stitching will be done later.

Cutting and Designing the Jeans Unit

1. Press the top of the jeans and cut off to the depth of the front zipper (10″ on the sample jacket). The remaining jeans fabric can be used for embellishment purposes. Carefully rip off the back pockets; set aside for possible use later.

Cut the jeans at the base of the front zipper.

Carefully remove the back pockets.

2. Machine-baste the shoulder seams and side seams to fit the vest and to determine the placement and depth of the jeans unit at the bottom, taking into consideration the length of your center front vest zipper. Then remove the basting to continue the construction process.

3. Mark where you want the top finished edge of the jeans unit to come at the center front, side seams, and center back of the sweatshirt. Decide how long you want the jeans unit to be; cut it 1″ longer than that, for safety's sake, cutting right through the zipper.

DESIGN NOTE

Though I had initially allowed 10″, I decided on a 6″ depth for the jeans unit—so I cut it down to 7″ (adding the 1″ security margin).

Cut the jeans to the measurement you've calculated.

4. Pin and stitch the front jeans pockets closed, *using a denim needle* (size 100) in the machine. On the inside of the jeans, cut away the excess pocket fabric below the stitching.

Stitch the pockets shut using a denim needle.

Cut off the pockets on the inside.

5. Fit again to decide if the sweatshirt needs to be taken in at the hemline for a closer fit.

DESIGN NOTE

The jeans unit is quite heavy, and it won't be flattering if it's too big around. You'll want to take in the sweatshirt to a flattering circumference before you finalize the jeans unit.

At this stage, the vest is too large in the back.

A 3" tuck was made at the center back, flattened, and stitched in place at the lower edge.

6. The jeans unit will have a substantial curve when it is laid flat. This curve needs to be straightened so that the unit is a straight piece.

The natural curve of the jeans needs straightening.

7. Eliminate the curve by slashing at the center back seam and side seams, and by stitching vertical tucks next to the front fly zipper if needed. Slash right into the well of the seams on the unstitched side, *up to but not through* the waistband.

Slash at the center back seam all the way up to the waistband.

Slash and overlap the fabric at the side seams to straighten the jeans unit.

8. Compare the length of the cut jeans unit to the sweatshirt's bottom edge circumference. Adjust as necessary until the sections are equal.

9. Overlap and pin the topstitched seams over the corresponding cut edges (Step 7) until the jeans waistband lies in a straight line and the cut edge matches the sweatshirt circumference.

Cut, lap, and stitch so that the jeans unit is straight along its cut edge.

10. Stitch shut through the original topstitching on the jeans using a size 100 denim needle in the machine. You may need to skip over the bulky seam at the center back—just fuse it together instead of expecting your machine to go through *that* many layers of heavy denim.

tip

Don't expect your new side and center back seams to match those on the sweatshirt unless you are very lucky. Also, the jeans unit seams will be at subtle angles. That's just fine!

11. When everything seems to fit, cut off the excess denim on the inside of the overlapping sections.

Trim the excess denim on the wrong side.

Finalizing the Placement

1. Mark where the jeans unit will attach to the body of the vest at the center fronts and the side seams. Again, take into account the available jacket zipper length to make *sure* the sweatshirt plus the jeans unit is no longer than the zipper you have purchased for the jacket front.

2. At the center back, lower the placement line you marked earlier by ½˝. Chalk this new (more flattering) line. Position the top edge of Straight Fusible Stay Tape along this line and fuse. Cut off the sweatshirt 2˝ below the stay tape.

Stabilize the new placement line and cut the sweatshirt 2˝ below the tape.

tip

The extra 2˝ of sweatshirt length inside the vest serves to support the heavy jeans unit.

3. Fuse Straight Fusible Stay Tape to the *right* side of the center fronts right along the edges.

Fuse stay tape on the outside of the center front edges.

4. Pin the jeans unit to the vest to make sure that the front fly zipper edges of the jeans unit align with the cut edges of the vest center fronts and that the top edges of the jeans unit match up across the center front. Unpin to continue.

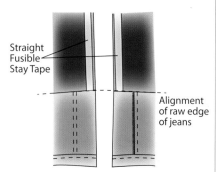

Check the jeans unit against the lower edge of the vest. The center front edges of the jeans unit and the vest must line up.

Finishing the Yoke Embellishment

By integrating denim, seams, or other features leftover from the jeans, complete the design of the front and back yokes.

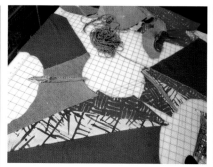

Front and back yokes with denim fabric and details integrated

1. Finish the fabric embellishment for the back yoke and couch yarns at the intersections of the fabric pieces. Refer to Couching Basics (page 24). Follow the directions for Stabilizing the Neckline (page 15).

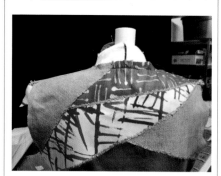

Finish the back yoke with fabric and yarn.

2. Finish the front yokes by couching yarns along the fabric edges and adding topstitched seams from the jeans scraps.

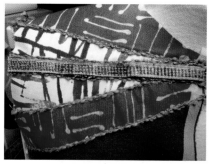

Finish embellishing the right front yoke.

Finish the left front yoke.

3. Staystitch the front neckline edges. Finish the shoulder and side seams with serging or long and wide 3-step zigzag stitching. Press the side seams toward the back.

4. Follow the instructions for Wrapped Band Finishing (page 19), applying these measurements:

- Cut the center front bands 3″ wide and 1½″ longer than the center front *sweatshirt edge*.

- Stitch the bands to the sweatshirt fronts with ⅝″ seams.

- *Stop* before stitching down the wrapped band on the outside so that you can add an accent strip.

Stitch the band to the front edge.

5. Cut the accent strip 1½″ wide from your second fabric, the same length as the band. Press in half lengthwise, wrong sides together. Lay this strip on the right side of the band that wraps the front, aligning the raw edges. Stitch together with a ¼″ seam.

Stitch the folded accent strip to the front band. The photo shows the band extended from inside the vest.

6. Wrap and press the combined front band / accent strip around the center front edge, letting the accent strip flip into place alongside the band. Pin in place.

Wrap the front edge with the front band / accent strip.

7. Repeat the process for the other front edge.

8. Secure the edges and embellish by couching yarn on each side of the accent strip.

Couch yarn along the edges.

Attaching the Jeans Unit

1. Lap and pin the *wrong* side of the jeans unit onto the *right* side of the vest bottom, just covering the stay tape and placing the pins parallel to the raw edge.

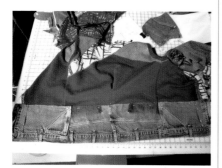

Lap the jeans unit over the stay tape and pin in place.

2. Stabilize the inside bottom edge of the sweatshirt by applying Straight Fusible Stay Tape to the right side (outside).

3. To nicely finish the inside sweatshirt edge, cut a 2″-wide strip of your darker fabric the length of the inside sweatshirt edge plus 1″. With right sides together and leaving ½″ of the strip extending at each front edge, stitch the fabric to *only the sweatshirt* using a ½″ seam.

4. Fold in the ends of the fabric at the center front edges and wrap the edge of the sweatshirt with the banding. Press under the long raw edge of the fabric and stitch through the sweatshirt (not the jeans unit) to finish the banding.

Fold in the ½″ ends and press under the free edge.

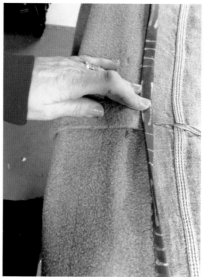

Wrap the banding around the sweatshirt edge and stitch.

5. Recheck the horizontal and vertical alignment of everything in the front—especially checking that the jeans unit edges align across the center front at the top and the bottom.

Check the alignment across the center front.

6. Zigzag stitch the jeans unit to the vest along the top, raw edge of the jeans on the right side. Couch yarn to cover the stitching.

Cover the stitching with couched yarn.

7. Alter and reattach the pockets to the back jeans unit, as you wish.

If your plan is to wear this vest with jeans, pockets on both the vest and on the jeans might be overkill. Consider this before adding pockets.

Inserting the Zipper

1. Pin the zipper to the center front edges so that the teeth are exposed. Stitch through all the layers ¼″ from the bound center front edges of the jacket.

2. Couch yarn down the center fronts on each side of the zipper. You should now have 3 slenderizing vertical lines of yarn on each side of the center front.

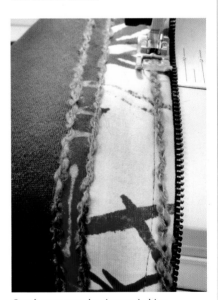

Couch yarn over the zipper stitching.

Adding Armhole Ribbings

1. Stitch each vest armhole ⅝″ from the edge, forcing the shoulder and underarm seam allowances toward the back. Trim the seam allowances to ¼″.

2. Cut the seam allowances from the cuff ribbings, leaving folded ribbings that are approximately 2″ wide. Open up the ribbings and cut in half lengthwise, yielding 4 pieces 2″ wide.

3. Sew 2 pairs of strips together across the short ends with ¼″ seams to create 2 armhole ribbing pieces. Grade the seam allowances, cutting one side of the seam allowance narrower. Press the seams open. Press each piece in half lengthwise.

Trim one side of the seam allowance and press the strip in half lengthwise.

4. Measure the arm opening along the stitching line. If both armholes don't measure the same, just take the average. Multiply by 0.66 to find the ribbing length you need.

5. Mark your measuring tape at the length you worked out in Step 4. Fold the tape end back to that line and mark the fold line. Match that line on the tape—the halfway point of your ribbing length—to the seam on the ribbing unit. Then mark the ribbing at the start of the tape and at the Step 4 length.

6. Open the ribbing. With right sides together, match the end marks and stitch a ¼″ seam. Grade the seam allowances.

Stitch each ribbing into a ring.

7. Match the ribbing seams to the side and shoulder seams on the vest, placing the shorter, trimmed right side of the ribbing to the wrong side of the armhole. Stretch the ribbing to match the armhole and pin in place, distributing the armhole fullness equally. Stitch a ¼˝ seam with the ribbing on top.

8. With the seam allowance pressed toward the ribbing, flip the free half of the ribbing over the seam to the *outside* of the vest; pin. Zigzag stitch (2 width, 3 length on my machine), using monofilament in the needle. Steam press.

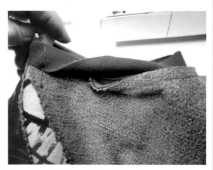

Turn the ribbing to the right side and pin in place.

9. Couch yarn to cover the stitching. Twist 2 yarns together if necessary to completely cover the edge, leaving yarn tails at the underarm as you begin and end your stitching. Bury the yarn ends on the inside, using a darning needle, as described in Couching Basics (page 24).

Couch yarn over the stitching, starting at the underarm seam.

Making the Collar

1. Measure the neckline at the stay stitching and multiply that figure by 0.66 to find the ribbing length you need (neckline length × 0.66 = ribbing length).

2. Trim the seam from the bottom sweatshirt ribbing, leaving ribbing that is 2˝–2¼˝ wide.

3. Fold the ribbing in half lengthwise and make a curved edge at one end of the ribbing, shaping the curve along the cut edge of the ribbing and leaving the folded edge longer.

4. As shown, fold the ribbing crosswise and use the cut curved end as a template to cut an identical curve at other end, measuring so that the ribbing length from one long tip to the other along the fold line will be the measurement calculated in Step 1.

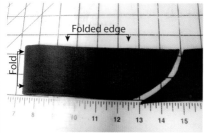

Cut a curve in the ribbing, with the folded side remaining the long edge.

5. Attach the neck ribbing the same way you attached the armhole ribbing in Step 7 (above left). Match the center of the ribbing length to the center back of the sweatshirt neckline. Couch yarn to cover as in Step 9 (above center).

Finish attaching the neckline ribbing.

Distinctive

Designed and made by Londa Rohlfing

Materials

- Basic Supplies (page 7)

- Sweatshirt (size 2XL), 80% cotton / 20% polyester

- 3 coordinating fabrics to blend with the sweatshirt *without* strong contrast:

  - 1 yard Fabric A (the lime background on the sample jacket)

  - ¾ yard Fabric B, preferably with a background color the same as the sweatshirt color (the lime circle print on the sample jacket)

  - ¾ yard Fabric C, a dark value to match the sweatshirt (black with ecru stripe effect on the sample jacket)

- 2 yards Fabric D for the neckline and front band, close to the sweatshirt in color (black silk dupioni on the sample jacket)

- ½ yard polar fleece for lengthening the body (this gets covered, so any color will work)

- ½ yard woven fusible interfacing for collar and cuffs

- 2 yards fusible web ½" wide

- 4 yards Straight Fusible Stay Tape

- Yarn for embellishing (I used a shiny yarn to tie in with the sheen of the black silk dupioni)

- 4½ yards zipper coil trim (ZipR by Kandi), or more for sizes 14 and up

- 1 yard of 1"-wide sport elastic

- 1 large button, approximately 1½" diameter

- Large pants hook and eye for waist closure (*optional*)

Getting Started

Method 2 must be used for fitting and constructing this jacket, so use pattern pieces 1, 2, 3, and 6. Follow the steps for Preparing the Sweatshirt (page 8). Follow the front neckline as designated on pattern piece 6 for this design. Position the pattern pieces on the available fabric to get as much body length as you can. The shoulder and yoke areas will be covered with fabric, so you can piece as needed to obtain the length you desire.

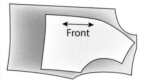

Place the patterns to provide the greatest possible jacket length.

The fabric piecing design and back belt placement will be determined by the natural waist location.

Measure to find these waist lengths and mark them on the pattern:

- Length from the shoulder at the neckline to the waist in front

- Center back length from the natural neckline to the waist

Adding Length

If you want to make your jacket longer than the sweatshirt fabric allows, here's how to do it.

1. Cut out the front and back pieces, making them as long as possible. Straighten the hemline edges.

2. Stabilize the hem edges by applying Straight Fusible Stay Tape on the *right* side of the fabric.

3. From the polar fleece, cut straight-grain pieces (so that any give in the cross grain of the polar fleece runs the depth of the extension piece) to extend the jacket to the length you want, *plus 2˝* for safety's sake.

4. Seam the extensions to the sweatshirt by overlapping the sweatshirt fabric on *top* of the fleece and stitching together with a large and wide zigzag stitch through the fusible stay tape.

Lap the tape-stabilized sweatshirt over the fleece and then zigzag stitch. The polar fleece will be trimmed to an exact length later.

Designing the Front Fabric Sections

> ### DESIGN NOTE
>
> *This is fun design work! My directions for arranging the fabric areas leave some "naked" sweatshirt fabric that gives the eye a "place to rest," to use design language. It's not necessary to cut your fabrics on the straight grain—the placement of the design motifs is more important. Mark off areas with string until you like the arrangement; then chalk the lines right onto the sweatshirt fabric. Some design hints:*
>
> ■ Lose pounds by placing darker-value colors at the sides and hips, as I did on my jacket.
>
> ■ Avoid strong patterns at the bust points. Mark the bust points on the sweatshirt and then avoid placing bold designs or horizontal lines (fabric seams) at that level.
>
> ■ Select a stronger design fabric for the right shoulder, since we tend to "read" garments from left to right, the same way we read the printed word.

1. Use the diagrams below as a guide to fabric selection and shape if you wish to create a jacket like the one that's pictured. *Cut all pieces ½˝ larger on all sides* than the desired finished dimensions. Measurements given are approximate for a medium size.

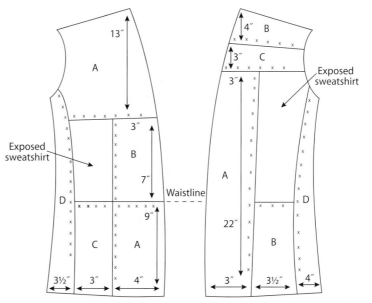

Jacket front: Measurements are approximate finished fabric pieces. Edges marked with X's are folded under ½˝ for a clean finish.

These photographs illustrate how I decided what fabric to use and where to use it.

1. This showed me that a high-contrast fabric—the light background with dark swirls—would draw too much attention to the areas where it was used.

2. Without the light fabric, the look is much improved.

3. Whoops—I surely don't want that big gray motif directly on the right bust point!

4. I wanted to see how the belt would affect the design.

5. How would the neckline look with the black silk dupioni bordered by zipper trim?

2. Cut your fabric pieces and arrange according to your design. Note that in the layout diagrams, edges to be turned under ½˝ are designated with X's and the adjacent fabric edges slide ½˝ under these folded edges. You may want to baste the front and back sections together at the shoulders for this design process.

3. If you basted the shoulder seams, now unstitch them to complete the design areas. Attach the fabric areas to the sweatshirt base, following the motifs in the prints with free-motion stitching. Rows of straight stitching also work well. The stitching "quilts" the fabric to the sweatshirt base.

For the "quilted" free-motion stitching, adjust the sewing machine as follows:

- Monofilament thread in the needle, polyester thread in the bobbin
- Lowered upper tension
- Feed dogs down and free-motion darning foot attached

For the folded edges of the overlays, use a zigzag stitch with a teeny width and regular stitch length (about 1 wide and 3 long on my machine) at the fabric intersections. Trim threads well on both sides of the pieces as you work.

4. After stitching, simply trim the fabric even with the sweatshirt base along the edges of the jacket pieces. Stitch the free edges of the overlays to the sweatshirt ¼" from the outer edges.

5. Couch yarn between fabric sections and where the fabric meets the sweatshirt base, following the instructions for Couching Basics (page 24). Start with the horizontal edges. (The sample jacket uses a single yarn for these.) Then couch the vertical edges, emphasizing these lines for a slimming effect. (The sample jacket uses 2 yarns twisted together.)

Use twisted yarns to couch the vertical edges.

Designing and Making the Back

1. Design the back side sections to intersect with the back yoke. Piece, stitch, and couch the back yoke fabric sections the same way you did the jacket front sections.

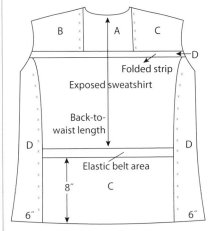

Jacket back: Measurements are approximate finished fabric pieces. Edges with X's are folded under ½" for a clean finish.

2. Finish the lower edge of the back yoke with an accent band cut from Fabric D. Measure across the lower edge of the back yoke, cut a strip 2½" × this length, and press in half lengthwise wrong sides together. Align the cut edges of the band with the bottom edge of the right side of the yoke; pin in place. Stitch with a ¼" seam, turn down the folded band edge, and press.

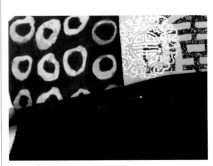

Stitch, flip down, and press the back accent band.

3. Couch yarn in the well of the seam at the top edge of the band.

4. Fit the jacket to determine the back waistline location. Mark with a pin and chalk the waistline across the center back section.

5. Cut the remaining back fabric sections, including the side backs and center lower back, from the dark-value Fabrics C and D. Extend the lower center back section up to the chalked waistline.

Dark sides and dark fabric over the derriere are flattering and slimming! The side pieces are cut from black silk Fabric D, and the back is dark cotton, Fabric C. In the photo, the lower back fabric is not yet added.

6. From the front side, "quilt" with vertical lines of stitching to attach the vertical side back and lower back fabric sections to the base sweatshirt fabric and fleece extension. Use an integrated dual-feed or walking foot on your machine, if available, and use monofilament thread in the needle.

As seen from the inside of the jacket, fabrics are stitched to the sweatshirt and fleece base with vertical stitching lines, using monofilament thread in the top thread.

7. Staystitch the back neckline; then pull the upper needle thread to adjust as needed, referring to Stabilizing the Neckline (page 15). Use a steam iron to shrink in excess fullness.

Staystitch and steam shrink the back neckline.

Gathering the Back

1. Measure the distance between the side back fabric pieces at the waistline. From Fabric D, cut a 2½"-wide casing strip that length *plus* 1" (for ½" seams at each end).

2. Press under ¼" along both long edges of the strip.

3. On the outside of the jacket back, align the top of the folded strip edge with the top edge of the center back fabric section. With the raw edge of the casing pointing toward the center of the jacket, pin one end of the casing strip to the edge of the left side back. Stitch in place across the end of the fabric casing in the well of the side back seam with a ¼" seam. Repeat on the right side to attach the other end of the casing strip, leaving the long folded edges of the casing free.

Attach the end of the casing strip at the side back edge of the center back fabric section.

4. Determine the length of sport elastic—stretched—that you need to span and gather the back in a flattering way. Cut a piece of elastic ½" *longer* than that.

tip

The sample jacket used a finished elastic measurement of 10" (therefore I cut it 10½" long) to span the 13½" distance between side back sections at the waist.

5. Securely stitch one end of the elastic in place underneath the loose casing, using a ¼" seam. Repeat to attach the elastic on the other end.

Stitch the end of the elastic in place.

The elastic has been attached at both ends, under the loose casing.

6. Pin to mark the centers of the casing strip, the elastic, and the back section. Match the centers and pin together. Stitch vertically across the casing strip at the marked center, stitching through all 3 layers.

Mark the centers, pin together, and then stitch across to secure.

7. Stretch to stitch the casing top and bottom edges to the jacket, taking care *not* to stitch through the elastic.

Stitch the folded edges of the casing, leaving the elastic free.

8. Using a long stitch length (5 on my machine), stretch and stitch horizontally along the center of the casing, stitching through everything *including* the elastic. Engage the needle-down function if your machine has it. Hover a steam iron over this elasticized area to steam shrink. Let the fabric cool before moving the fabric.

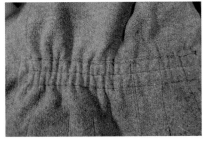

Casing stitching from inside the jacket

Assembling the Jacket

1. Stitch the jacket shoulder seams, easing the back into the fronts—which are "stayed" by virtue of the fabric on top.

2. Stitch the side seams. (Note that because the front and back pieces were cut as long as the fabric allowed, the tops of the fleece extensions may not line up across the side seams.) Check the fit.

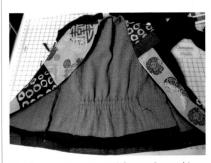

The fleece extensions at right aren't equal in length, but the bottom edges align.

3. Serge or zigzag the side and shoulder seam allowances. Press toward the back.

4. Try on the jacket to decide the finished length you want at the front, sides, and back. (Design the back to be a bit longer than the side seams to create a nice silhouette from behind.) Pin up the hem and press. Do not expect an equidistant hem allowance!

5. Allowing for a ½″ seam allowance at the bottom, mark and trim off the excess hem allowance.

6. Fuse Straight Fusible Stay Tape to the bottom edge on the *outside* of the fleece extensions or on the sweatshirt itself if no extra length has been added.

7. If fleece was added to increase the jacket length, measure on the inside to determine the fabric depth needed to cover the fleece added for more length. Add 1″ to that measurement.

8. From Fabric D, cut a facing strip the width from Step 7 and the length of the lower jacket circumference. It's best to cut this strip on the bias so that it can be shaped to the bottom edge and steam-shaped at the top edge as necessary. (However, because I used a lightweight silk for the facing, I did not cut mine on the bias.) Fold one long edge under ½″ and press.

9. Clip the side seam allowance of the jacket ½˝ from the bottom edge and force the seam allowances in opposite directions above and below the clip to balance the bulk.

10. Pin the right side of the unturned facing strip edge to the right side of the jacket at the bottom edge. Stitch a ½˝ seam.

Stitch the facing strip to the bottom edge of the jacket.

11. Press the facing strip to the wrong side of the jacket. Take tucks in the facing if necessary to make it fit at the upper facing strip edge. Apply strips of fusible web to secure facing to the inside of the jacket along the uppermost edge of the facing strip.

12. On the right side of the jacket, stitch in-the-ditch of the side seams and along any couched seams to hold the facing strip securely in place.

Stitch over side seams and couched seams to secure the facing.

13. Couch yarn along the vertical lines of the side back sections.

14. Attach the sleeves to the jacket according to the directions for Setting Sleeves (page 18).

Making the Belt

tip

For the sample jacket, a 2XL sweatshirt yielded 48˝ of lower-edge ribbing to use for the belt. The belt length gets adjusted at the end opposite the buttonhole as the ribbing is caught in the neckline finish.

1. Trim the seam allowance from the bottom sweatshirt ribbing, referring to Preparing the Sweatshirt (page 8).

2. Press under ¾˝ on one end. Center and apply a square of fusible interfacing on the wrong side of the folded ribbing end, as shown in the photo (below). Mark the buttonhole size needed for the button you've chosen. (Make the buttonhole plenty big!)

Fuse interfacing to the wrong side of the folded ribbing end and mark the buttonhole size.

DESIGN NOTE

As an alternative closure, you can stitch a decorative button onto the right front along with a hook-and-eye closure. Attach a large pants hook underneath the right front and the straight eye portion on the left front. If you decide on this treatment to eliminate the buttonhole (which is a challenge to make!), just skip the buttonhole directions.

3. Hand baste along the button-hole center and ends (no knots) with contrasting thread so that the size will be obvious from the right side.

Baste the buttonhole location with contrasting thread.

4. Press the long cut edges of the ribbing to the wrong side so that they meet at the original fold line of the ribbing. On the wrong side, zigzag stitch (5 long, 4.5 wide stitch settings on my machine) down the center of the belt to catch both long edges. Be sure that the zigzag is wide enough to catch both long edges of the belt.

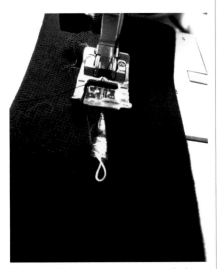

Zigzag stitch down the center to attach the butted ribbing edges.

tip ....

Make a practice buttonhole in a piece of cuff ribbing that you've prepared the same way. Consult the machine manual for how to cord a buttonhole and, if applicable, how to make a buttonhole larger than the prepro-grammed sizes.

5. Work a machine buttonhole, cording it by stitching over a heavy thread (or 2 strands of regular thread) to keep it from stretching. Cording helps the buttonhole maintain its shape, as does the interfacing. Remove the hand basting threads.

Make a corded machine buttonhole.

6. Fit the jacket to determine the length and exact location of the belt. Mark an attractive placement for your body; the belt should cover the elastic fitting gathers in the back. Pull the belt just tightly enough to cinch in the jacket a bit for a flattering fit. This is not a close fit, as the jacket is somewhat bulky at this spot. The finished edge on the right front (the end with the buttonhole) should extend a generous 1½″ *beyond* the cut edge

of the jacket front—so that it will extend over the top of the front neckline band. On the left front, cut the belt end flush with the center front edge. Pin the belt in place and stitch to secure the left front end so that it will be caught in the neckline/center front band.

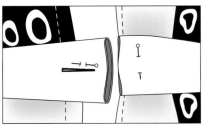

Pin the belt in place.

7. On the belt, mark the side seam and center back locations.

8. Embellish the belt however you wish. Zipper coil tape was used on the sample jacket, attached using the zipper foot to stitch close to the coil as shown.

Use the zipper foot to attach zipper coil, bending the trim flush with the right end of the belt and stitching on either side of the buttonhole.

9. Cut away any trim bulk in the seam allowance at the belt end so that you will be able to attach the front band. Couch yarn in the center of the zipper tape, if you wish.

Cut away the zipper coil from the seam allowance.

tip

To couch the yarn down the center of the zipper tape, I needed to use a blind hem stitch of 5 width on my machine because of where the zipper coil's bulk forced the foot to ride.

10. Attach the belt to the jacket at the side seams and the center back by stitching across it through all layers—by machine, if possible, or by hand tacking.

Finishing the Neckline

1. From Fabric D, cut a band 5″ wide and 2″ longer than the length of the continuous center front and back neckline edge. Piece if necessary, locating the seaming in an inconspicuous place. Interface with fusible interfacing on the *wrong* side. With wrong sides together, press in half lengthwise.

Cut the neckline band, interface it, and press it in half lengthwise.

tip

To reduce bulk in the seam allowance area, I always cut interfacing 1″ narrower than the piece to which it is being attached. Never interface over a seam; instead, cut the interfacing and slip it under each seam allowance.

2. Pin the right side of one band edge to the wrong side of the jacket edge, leaving 1″ excess band length at each lower front hem end. Stitch in place with a ⅜″ seam.

Stitch one edge of the band to the wrong side of the jacket.

3. Fold up the excess at each lower center front edge. Press ⅜″ under on the long free edge of the band. Fold in the ends of the band flush with the hemline of the jacket. Pin in place.

Press up the excess at the ends and ⅜″ in along the free long edge.

4. Turn the band to the outside so the center crease from Step 1 becomes the center band edge. Stitch the folded edge to the jacket body, inserting the zipper coil or other trim under the folded edge as you stitch.

Insert trim under the folded edge and stitch through all the layers.

tip

At the bust level, expect to have to ease in a bit of extra length. Use an even-feed foot or a feature on your machine to assist you in doing this.

5. Couch yarn over the stitching as desired. Slipstitch the open bottom edges of the band at the center front lower edges.

6. Turn in the very ends of the belt at the buttonhole right front end so that it is flush with the finished front band. Slipstitch this folded end closed.

Creating the Closure

DESIGN NOTE

Take great care when cutting this buttonhole open that you do not cut through the very front fold of the front band. This combined thickness of belt and front band buttonholes led me to suggest the option of a nonfunctional, purely decorative button in combination with a hook and eye (see Design Note, page 90).

1. Sew the button to the left front in the center of the waist/front band. Make a thread shank long enough to accommodate the thickness of the left front and waist bands. Work a buttonhole stitch over the thread shank to make it extra nice and durable.

Stitch on the button with a generous thread shank.

2. Mark and work a buttonhole in the right front band, just below the buttonhole in the belt. The button will actually button through this buttonhole and the buttonhole in the belt.

3. Fit the jacket to make sure everything is in place. On the right front, slipstitch the very front edge of the belt to the neckline band.

Hand slipstitch the loose end of the belt to the neck band.

Making the Cuffs

1. From Fabric A, cut 2 *bias* cuffs 6″ wide and 2″ *longer* than the sleeve circumference at the bottom edge. Press in half lengthwise with wrong sides together.

2. Fit the jacket to determine the finished sleeve length you want. Follow the steps for Wrapped Band Finishing (page 19), integrating the measurements and steps below to lengthen the sleeves by 2″ (for a different cuff length, adjust accordingly).

Cut and interface half of each cuff piece.

3. Stabilize the edge of each sleeve with Straight Fusible Stay Tape fused to the outside of the sleeve edges. Then stitch the *right* side of the uninterfaced cuff edge to the *wrong* side of the sleeve.

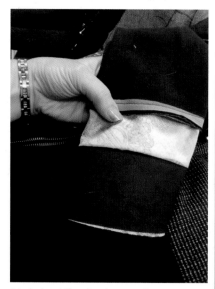

Stitch the cuff to the sleeve as shown.

4. Press the cuff down and away from the sleeve. Flip the interfaced portion up, over the sleeve edge to the outside of the sleeve. Press under ¼″ on the free edge. Pin in place on the jacket sleeve and attach with a narrow zigzag stitch (3 long, 0.5 wide on my machine). Alternatively, since the cuffs were cut on the bias grain and won't ravel, this edge can be left unfinished. Cover the edge with couched yarn if you don't add the optional accent band (following procedure).

Adding an Accent Band

1. From Fabric C, cut 2 pieces 2½″ wide and 2″ longer than the upper cuff circumference. From Fabric B, cut 2 pieces 2″ wide and the same length.

2. Press each piece in half lengthwise with wrong sides together. Layer a Fabric B piece on top of a Fabric C piece, raw edges aligned, and baste together ¼″ from the raw edges to create an accent band unit. Repeat with the remaining 2 pieces.

Align the raw band edge and baste together.

3. Butt the raw edges of an accent band, layered side facing down, against the cuff edge. Turning the end in as you begin, stitch the band to the sleeve, overlapping the ends as you finish stitching.

Attach the accent band, right side down and butted against the cuff edge.

4. Press and flip the accent band into place over the cuff edge. Couch yarn in the well of the seam next to the sweatshirt sleeve, burying the yarn ends as described in Couching Basics (page 24). Stitch vertically through all of the layers to secure at the underarm seam, marked in the photo with a pin.

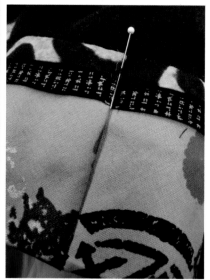

Flip the accent band into place and stitch at the underarm seam.

About the Author

Londa can't remember *not* sewing! Taught by her mother during Londa's early years, she was sewing most of her wardrobe by her early teens. Earning a B.S. degree in home economics from the University of Illinois was a natural education pathway, leading to positions in interior design, managing a craft store, and years of custom dressmaking from home while her children were young. She added to her skills with subsequent training in color analysis and wardrobe styling.

Along the way, Londa became enchanted with heirloom sewing and its creative possibilities. After attending a business school at Martha Pullen School of Art Fashion in 1988, she launched her women's pattern line featuring heirloom sewing: Londa's Elegant Creations. In 1990 she opened her own retail storefront, Londa's Sewing Etc., offering fine fabrics, quilting, classes, and sewing machines.

After thirteen years, Londa switched gears to become an Internet-based business, Londa's Creative Threads (www.londas-sewing.com), through which she strives to "offer top-quality service, education, and sewing products with passion as a fellow seamstress, teacher,

and designer." She travels extensively, teaching creative sewing at shops, sewing expos, and sewing guilds and sharing her obsession for transforming comfortable sweatshirts into stylish jackets and creating embellishing T-shirts.

In 2009 Londa developed her Talking Patterns to empower and encourage her customers as they sew, offering online photographs and personal recorded directions for each step of her jacket creation process. She has also published a book with the same Talking Pattern format and has produced several DVDs.

Londa's work has been published in *Creative Needle, Sewing Savvy, American Sewing Guild's Notions,* and *Sew Beautiful* magazines. Her creations have also been included in Martha Pullen's *Heirloom Sewing for Women* and in *Sweatshirts with a Twist* by DRG. She has been a featured designer on Pfaff's website www.nowsewing.net and the PBS television series *It's Sew Easy.*

Notions and tools mentioned in this book, as well as technique tutorials, can be ordered from the author at her website, Londa's Creative Threads (www.londas-sewing.com).

Businesses may contact Londa to obtain information about wholesale sources for USA Comfort Color sweatshirts.

Londa and her husband of 40 years, Charley, are the proud parents of Jeff and Carmen and love being grandparents to number one grandson, Cole. They live in central Illinois.

Resources

Fabrics (*InVested, Distinctive*):
    www.marciaderse.com

Zippers (*InVested*):
    www.ghees.com

Great Titles and Products

from C&T PUBLISHING and stashBOOKS.

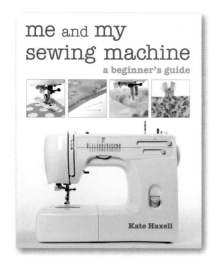

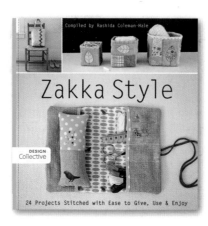

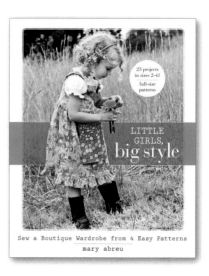

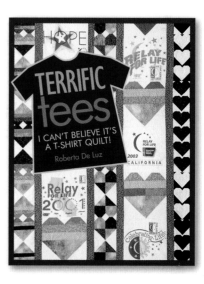

Available at your local retailer or **www.ctpub.com** *or* **800-284-1114**

For a list of other fine books from C&T Publishing, visit our website
to view our catalog online.

C&T PUBLISHING, INC.

P.O. Box 1456
Lafayette, CA 94549
800-284-1114

Email: ctinfo@ctpub.com
Website: www.ctpub.com

C&T Publishing's professional photography services are now available to
the public. Visit us at www.ctmediaservices.com.

Tips and Techniques can be found at www.ctpub.com > Consumer
Resources > Quiltmaking Basics: Tips & Techniques for Quiltmaking & More

For quilting supplies:

COTTON PATCH

1025 Brown Ave.
Lafayette, CA 94549
Store: 925-284-1177
Mail order: 925-283-7883

Email: CottonPa@aol.com
Website: www.quiltusa.com

Note: Fabrics shown may not be currently available, as fabric
manufacturers keep most fabrics in print for only a short time.